POLITICS AND ETHNICITY: POLITICAL ANTHROPONYMY IN NORTHERN GHANA

FOCUS ON CIVILIZATIONS AND CULTURES

Additional books in this series can be found on Nova's website under the Series tab.

Additional E-books in this series can be found on Nova's website under the E-book tab.

AFRICAN POLITICAL, ECONOMIC, AND SECURITY ISSUES

Additional books in this series can be found on Nova's website under the Series tab.

Additional E-books in this series can be found on Nova's website under the E-book tab.

FOCUS ON CIVILIZATIONS AND CULTURES

POLITICS AND ETHNICITY: POLITICAL ANTHROPONYMY IN NORTHERN GHANA

ABDULAI SALIFU

Nova Science Publishers, Inc.
New York

For permission to use material from this book please contact us:
Telephone 631-231-7269; Fax 631-231-8175
Web Site: http://www.novapublishers.com

NOTICE TO THE READER

LIBRARY OF CONGRESS CATALOGING-IN-PUBLICATION DATA
Salifu, Abdulai.
  Politics and ethnicity : political anthroponymy in Northern Ghana /
Abdulai Salifu.
    p. cm.
  Includes bibliographical references and index.
  ISBN 978-1-61122-139-8 (hardcover)
  1. Music--Social aspects--Ghana--Dagomba. 2. Dagbani (African
people)--Music--History and criticism. 3. Laudatory poetry,
African--History and criticism. I. Title.
  ML3760.S22 2010
  305.896'35--dc22   2010037377

Published by Nova Science Publishers, Inc. † New York

CONTENTS

DEDICATION

Dedicated to my parents, Nakɔha and Jahima, who encouraged me to stay in school, even though they never got the opportunity to go to school.

PREFACE

In this work I set out to give interpretations of performances, events, and verbal phenomena. I am neither an expert in this arena of praise naming/singing, nor do I claim any ingenuity in the art of praise interpretation. This statement is neither a disclaimer of knowledge nor an admission of incompetence, but a genuine statement of one stepping out into a novel terrain, a part of which was previously unknown to him, and indeed to many others. Much of the material appears to be common place ones and have been taken for granted. Interpretation is not as clear-cut as it may appear, and when we engage in interpretation we attempt to properly describe some object or situation in which we have an interest and are unsure about which of several available analytical methods we should use to explain it. My interpretation is thus a product of thought in a preliminary stage of consciously thinking of, and grasping a phenomenon, a praise naming tradition, and deciding, not only *how* to describe and explain it, but *whether* it can be adequately described or explained at all.

I have tried as much as possible to render other people's narrative as well as my own explanations and descriptions. I basically cannot boast about "creating" what I report here. It is not an instantiation, but a report of what the unsung heroes, the drummers, have created and re-created over half a millennium. The discourse of praise singing is essentially figurative, and this leads to multiple descriptions, perspectives and points of view as to what a praise epithet really means. I give the bulk of the credit to the army of informants who graciously gave me very useful information, but I am liable for any lapses that may be in this write up.

I have tried to give lineal glosses of epithets where the texts are not so long, before giving the close translations; but where texts are too long I go directly to translations without the intervening glosses. Oftentimes some of the literal translations require further information because the sentences are figurative or proverbial appropriation of local idioms that non-Dagombas may not easily comprehend. Even as a native speaker, I still found it difficult to follow some portions of some narrations, due to dialectal differences between me and the performers, and also, some parts of the recordings were not clear enough. Dagbani is a tonal language and uses a phonetic alphabet. Most English phonemes are present in Dagbani, except /θ/ as in "thing", /ð/ as in "the", and the vowels, /æ/ as in "bat", /ʌ/ as in cut, /ə/ as in "father". The following are not found in English orthography and as such will be unfamiliar to the English speaker,

- "ɣ" a glottalized "g" usually occurring intervocalically in Dagbani,
- /ŋ/ as found at the end of the English word "sing",
- /ʒ/ as in the initial part of "genre"

It also has doubly articulated sounds like,

- "kp", "gb", "ŋm" (all three are non-English sounds), "ch" as in church, and /ny/ (a palatal nasal, as found in the French 'cognac')

My family has been very supportive and has had to sacrifice being with a husband, a father, a sibling, or a friend, to various constituents of my large extended Dagomba family. I cannot thank them enough for this sacrifice. The master drummer, Luŋa Alhassan Fuseini has been a teacher and a friend. I owe him a world of thanks. He sacrificed his evenings over the summer of 2007 to instruct me in Dagomba oral culture and praise singing, and in fact stopped short of initiating me into the drumming tradition. So too, do I thank my able research assistant Zosimli Lunnnaa Issah Yakubu, himself a young drummer, for not only recording performances for me, but also explaining drum lore to me.

This book sets out to investigate the praise poetry genre of the Dagombas of northern Ghana. The art of drumming, performed by court figures known as drummers, is at the heart of Dagomba culture, and is central to this book. How are the titles and accolades each naa "chief/king" goes by chosen? Why are they so proverbial in nature, and why do they taunt others? These questions, in addition to how we can channel panegyrics to positive uses, are the issues this book intends to address. This, I presume will help foster a cross-fertilization of ideas between the oral artists, their patrons, and academics; and also engender economic activity for the artists.

Chapter 1

INTRODUCTION

If you want to reward an ingrate ensure that you have one who is worse
than him/her (that is a drummer) to be a witness and eventually publicize the
event in the event that this ingrate lives up to his/her name and denies your
being the benefactor.

Anonymous Drummer

This opening statement is a popular adage used to describe the position of
the drummers[1] of Dagbon, who are the principal architects of the genre of
poetry we shall be looking at in this study. The Dagombas[2] constitute the
largest ethnic group in Northern Ghana[3] and they have a very rich oral
tradition. This pool of 'raw', 'untapped' literature is pleading to be exploited;
yet scholars have somehow so far failed to heed the plea. Dagombas (also
called Dagbamba (Dagbana SG)) an ethnic group from the Gur language
family of the Niger Congo language family, speak the Dagbani (or Dagbanli)
language. The Dagbaŋ (or Dagbon) Kingdom which is some 8082 square
miles in area, dates back to the fifteenth century, with its early warrior
equestrian ancestors coming into the present north-eastern location in modern
day Ghana, from the Chadic region, (see Fage 1978: 66). The Yaa Naa is the
King and overlord of the Dagbon nation, and he has an ensemble of musicians

---

[1] Christine Oppong 1973:54 describes the drummers, Lunsi, as "the court historians and
musicians, chroniclers of the past and recorders of the present."

[2] This is the largest ethnic group in Ghana, after the Akan community, and has a population of
about a million speakers throughout the West African country, Ghana.

[3] Ghana is a West African country of about twenty million people that is bordered on the east by
Togo, Cote d'Ivoire in the west, Burkina Faso in the north, and the Atlantic Ocean to the
south.

whose duty it is to praise as well as entertain him. Music and musicians are thus of paramount importance to Dagomba cosmology, because the King is at the core of the tradition, as he is the embodiment of the people's soul. The history of the Dagbon nation is invariably tied to the political history[4] of the Kingship. Every village and town has a chief who also has a team of elders to assist in his administration, modeled along the same lines as the King at Yendi, the Capital of the Dagbon nation (see map below).

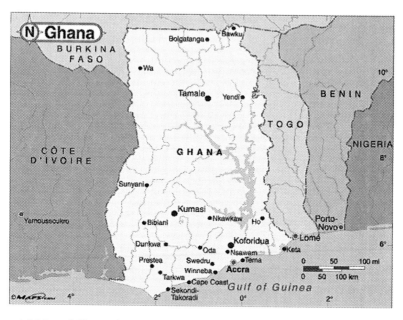

Figure 1.1 Map of Ghana (from Maps.com).

In the thesis for my Masters' degree, I wrote on *An Ethnography of Royal Discourse in Dagbon*. In that work I dwelt on the communicative situations at the court of the overlord of the Dagombas. The use of drums and praise singing /uttering was so profuse that I decided my next research should narrow down to analyzing the potency of the hour-glass drum, and the praise epithets that go along with the drummed messages. Personal observation has also informed me of the genre's potential of being used as a subversive tool. It is therefore my desire to look into how such a potent folkloric, sociocultural

---

[4] Martin Staniland 1975 gives a detailed account of this political history of Dagbon.

communicative system that should give a people an identity and a sense of solidarity can drive them to violence[5].

Davidson (1974:20), Vansina (1954:50), and Paredes (1994) maintain that even though it normally maintains stability and reinforces cultural traditions, folklore is potentially disruptive of the social order. This is the phenomenon I want to study among the *lunsi* "drummers", who are the praise singers of Dagbon. This drummer institution is believed to have been established under Dagomba King Nyaɣisi (1416-1432), grandson of Naa Gbewaa[6], who is the common ancestor of the Mole-Dagbani languages of Dagbanli, Mɔhili (Moori), Mampruli (Ŋmampruli), Nanunli, and Kusahili (Kusaal). Naa Nyaɣisi is regarded as the founder of modern Dagbon, and he moved the capital from Western Dagbon to Yendi in the east.

Praise poetry in Dagbon utilizes proverbs and nicknames, which are observed to have the potential of inviting conflict. A popular Dagomba adage has it that,

Ŋah' ŋahira nyɛla vu'bɔra, ŋah' baŋda nyɛla vu' bɔra
Proverb sayer be trouble-seeker, proverb-knower be trouble-seeker
Both the user of proverbs and the interpreter are trouble rousers

Praise names are proverbs which need to be interpreted. It is this interpretation that may serve as the sharp thorns that will prick others, or the 'soft' thorns that will pinch them to wake up to their responsibilities. Aristotle distrusts poetry because of this subversive potential. It has the potency to induce violent actions that in turn provide material for further poetic expressions. Yet, poetry is centrally placed in the scheme of events in the daily life of humans.

Typically, Dagombas are suspicious of the modern day formal set up, and would not entrust the training of their young to an 'outsider' whose ways they are unfamiliar with; little wonder it has only been in recent times traditional leaders (chiefs) have become literate in the western sense[7]. The colonial

---

[5] Such taunts, which royals relish, have led to many wars, and each new war is further grist for newer praise epithets.

[6] Gbewaa is to the Mole-Dagbani group of languages what Sunjata is to the Manding (a term used to collectively refer to the Mandinka of The Gambia and Guinea-Conakry, the Bambara of Mali and Senegal and the Dyula of Cote d'Ivoire; see Gordon Innes 1976: 1).

7 Islam came to them first, around the seventeenth century A.D, and they were comfortable with practicing a syncretic type of Islam in which they incorporated traditional rituals. The new Muslim converts used charms and other protective services rendered by the Muslim

British administrators had to compel chiefs, in the mid-twentieth century to send their children to school. The chief (King) is an embodiment of the culture, and is seen to have both physical and spiritual power. Before the advent of colonialism in Dagbon the chieftaincy institution was so rich that it satisfied all aspects of the people's everyday life. The palace was the center of the universe, and it had the drummers, who educated, informed, entertained, and recorded history, playing a key role in everyday life of the Dagbon state. The various court elders were practiced orators whose craft relied so much on proverb usage and praising their superiors. Even though Islam has a big influence, the traditional lore is given more preference. For example,

> A balima yee zav'yini so haʒi kɔbiga
> Your mercies please one better than Hajj hundred
> One line of praise is better than a hundred pilgrimages to Mecca,

was how a royal title aspirant responded to a question as to whether he would prefer performing the Muslim pilgrimage, *Hajj*, or the chieftaincy title. He chose to go with traditional royalty with all the praises that go with the position to being a 'mere' *Alhaj* X, the title a returnee from the pilgrimage to Mecca is addressed by.

AIM AND SCOPE

This work sets out to investigate the potential use of a verbal genre, *salima*, to subvert the social order among the royals of traditional Dagbon in particular, and within the entire ethnic group as a whole. *Salima* translates as 'praise' or 'stories', combining the senses of both reality and fantasy. I intend to address questions of how and why praise names are chosen, in addition to how panegyrics can be used to achieve positive ends. This, I hope, will help foster a cross-fertilization of ideas among the oral artists, their patrons, and academics. If we are able to capture this genre for the exemplar of great poetry that it is, it is my expectation that our enterprise will engender economic activity for the bards, serve as a rich pool of literature for the populace, as well as attract tourism to the land, especially at traditional festivals. It is ironic that

---

clerics, who also educated the children in the Quranic schools. The colonialist educators were seen as a Christian proselytizing force coming to capture their young.

I am advocating that a potentially conflict-inviting genre is one that will attract others to its performances. This is what it will seem like at first sight, but the allure of the pomp and pageantry of the traditional festivals is more inviting, and the benefits outweigh the potential risks. The book will also open up this esoteric body of art to the 'outside' world. Outside world here does not only denote one who is foreign to this ethnic group, but encompasses all who neither belong to the royal class nor are of the drummer caste (including drummers, *lunsi*, fiddlers, *goonjenima*, the timpani player *akarima,* or the flutists *yu' piɛbira*). There is an in-, and an out- group to be found in this dichotomy. A Dagomba who is not part of a particular royal lineage is as much an outsider as any other non-Dagomba. Privileges may however be extended to others whom each family decides to adopt as a member of their in-group.

There is a category of people in Dagbon who see the drummers' art as diversionary. They think it takes our minds away from present reality, to bask in the glory of a fantastic past, or give us the illusion of being able to achieve an unachievable future goal. This will equate with what Marxist theory calls *an opiate of the masses*, a social event that binds the participants in socially defined ways, what Alver (2005: 50) refers to as *Folklorism*, " an interest and idolizing of culture forms and cultural traits which belong to the past, especially to the older rural culture".

I do not subscribe to this point of view because praise names are a window through which we have access to the way the people perceive their universe. In Gramsci's (see Dundes: 131)[8] view, folklore, as typified by praise singing in our present context, 'provides a unique source for the study of worldview. ..., a conception of the world.' Among the Dagomba, an orator is one who, in addition to knowing where and when to speak, has diction that makes good use of proverbs and witty statements to coin praise names and accolades for both themselves and others. There are dance forms with names that are proverbial and targeted at others within the community. All these forms are targets for study in the proposed undertaking, in an effort to analyze proverbial language as targeted language. These names will either prick those who bear them to act in certain socially prescribed ways, or prick in order to hurt the feelings of some targeted audiences whom the name owner intends to affect in particular ways.

Praise poetry should uplift a people's spirits, and motivate them to achieve higher laurels. But, some of the praise epithets affluent and noble persons

---

[8] See Alan Dundes' International Folkloristics.

choose for themselves tend to be abusive, or cast insinuations at others, a tendency that can lead to conflicts. Other names employ profane words. Why is this so? Is a name that draws the wrath of another and has the potential to cause social upheaval worth possessing? Is this a liability to the society as a whole, a kind of "negative name", if it hurts the society? How can practitioners redirect their focus, so that praise names will serve positive ends, and not invite violence or social strife? These are questions I set out to find answers to in this book.

As already stated, the language of praise-poetry is condensed and proverbial. The proverb that a royal person takes (or accepts from his/her drummer) as his/her name is either witty or satiric of their foes or political rivals[9] who they might have beaten in the contest to ascend to their present political position, or title. Dagomba 'praise names' both bestow praise on their targets as well give indication of their ancestral lineage, and incidents in their careers. This fits the paradigm noted by Innes (1976: 22) to be common to African praise epithets. Names like,

> i. N daŋ ba nyabu, bɛ ku niŋ shɛli
> I precede them seeing, they NEG do anything
> I know them, so they cannot do anything harmful to me.

This epithet imputes that there is a diabolical character within sight that the speaker identified. This might induce the target audience to act in order to show that they can act.

> ii. X –nim dabari zaana
> X-PL deserted homes maker
> One who creates deserted houses in town X

tells of someone who killed people of town X, a stock phrase used by the bards to describe a patron as a brave warrior.

> iii. Ba, she ŋun nye o karimbaan bindi ni va o karimbaan bindi.
> Dog who that shits its arrogant feces will collect its arrogant feces
> The arrogant dog who defecates at a prohibited place will clean up its feces.

---

[9] Chieftaincy titles in Dagbon have always been contested between princes. They covet the position so much so that they see fellow contestants as enemies.

This third name calls the rival a proud dog who has himself to blame if the results of his actions come back to haunt him. This certainly is non complimentary.

> iv.Kambaŋ paɣa/ Guŋgɔna paɣ' bia, Naɣbiɛɣu
>
> Kambaŋ/ Guŋgɔna woman child, Naɣbiɛɣu
>
> Naɣbiɛɣu, the son of the woman from Diyali

This identifies the patron with his mother's town, Diyali, whose epithet is *Kambaŋ yili*.

Towns and villages also have their praise names (see example iv above), so that every citizen can in one way or the other have a praise epithet, to help boost their ego. There are praise names that center on conquests or victory in wars over other ethnic groups or towns. Recounting such painful and humiliating experiences before people from such origins or the descendants of these once vanquished groups can present potential conflict situations (as in ii above). The epic stories of Naa Luro (1554-1570), in which he defeats a Gonja King Kalɔɣisi Dajia and kills many people (personal communication), is one such experience the neighboring Gonja ethnic group has not forgotten, and up until now, there is still a state of mutual distrust between the two most dominant ethnic groups of Northern Ghana. It is upsetting if one takes a praise name that alludes to this historic event and flaunts it in the presence of another fellow whose forebears were the vanquished? I wonder how neighborly these two can be if one has praise epithets that do not respect the face concerns of the other (Goffman 1955), and these get repeated now and then, at festivals, funerals and other social milieus.

POTENTIAL BENEFITS

During my field trips to Yendi and its environs in 1998, I had unimpeded access to live drumming and praise-uttering sessions. I did not go to the Yendi area this time (in 2007) for there was still some tension between the two feuding royal families. However, I did not lack for seasoned bards, as they came from all over the Dagbaŋ to occasions in Tamale, the regional capital. Some of the drummers even agreed to instruct me in surrogate drum language interpretation. I soon learnt that a singer is not interrupted when he is chanting. In a live performance a member of an ensemble may cue a singer if he slips, by drumming the message to him. Taboos on when and how songs can be sung had to be observed, and as already mentioned some sacrifices of chickens were made before certain bits of narrations could be rendered, for spiritual fortification.

When I set out into the field, my major fear was how to do a balancing act and collect data from both Abudu and Andani sources, the two antagonistic factions of the Dagomba chieftaincy divide. This is a key element in any ethnographic inquiry in Dagbaŋ that has to do with chieftaincy and culture. One has to tread cautiously, in order to tap resources from these two sides without any suspicions of being a 'traitor', for as the saying in Dagbani goes, *a yibali mini a sim yi tɔɣisira nyin niŋmi siɣa* 'if your enemy and your friend are consorting, you need to tread with caution.'.

My original fear of treading cautiously was minimized by chance meetings with singers from both factions. I did not consciously go after singers sympathetic to any particular side of the political divide. I wanted to know from my sources: what praise names exist and qualify to be listed as *salima*? Who composes the praise name/title? When is the composition done? How does one save oneself from societal wrath in the event the name offends others? I also visited the Center for National Culture, Tamale, to see what resources they had, but did not get much information there. This encouraged me to persevere in my inquiry so that in future I, as a former literary arts representative of their governing board, could share some of my findings with them. The study will thus be of tremendous importance to them in their task of getting a data bank of cultural information of the Northern Region.

It is my ultimate goal that, "Names that Prick" will eventually be useful as a guide to achieving both intra- and inter- societal harmony. It will also be material for further cross-cultural studies. Festivals could not be celebrated in Dagbon prior to the burial of the late murdered King in 2006, because of the possibility of sparking a conflict. Where there is a festival in Dagbon there must be praise-poetry, which can inflame passions. These festivals (especially, *Damba* and *Buɣum*) have been occasions where thousands of visitors, from Europe and America mostly, flock to see these celebrations of poetry, music, and dance. It is my ardent wish to see this come back, for it builds a bridge to link up peoples who have been separated in time and space. It is heart-warming to see Africans from the Diaspora and other visitors all engage in celebration of poetry, music and dance.

Chapter 2

A NOTE ABOUT METHOD

I essentially view praise singing as a process of communication, which Hymes (1975) notes as being central to "Folklore as Communication." Performance is primarily seen as an overt manifestation of the speaker's verbal knowledge and behavior. Contemporary folklore combines knowledge of traditional material with elements in the emergent social event. This view conceives of performance as context dependent, emergent and arising within a particular context. Labov (1966) observes that cultural behavior is interpretable and reportable. This is complemented by Hymes adding a third dimension, the repeatable, to these two. Based on this proposition, we shall engage in the analyses of material presented in this essay looking at these three dimensions, classifying and explaining; doing and performing; and reporting and describing, representing the three aspects.

Like van Gennep (1873-1957) who considered folklore to be 'living' in distinction to previous notion of the discipline as one of 'dead' survivals from the past I do not start this enquiry as a collector of material that is on the verge of dying, getting corrupted, and thus needing to be captured on paper before it is lost to eternity. I see the art as an everyday phenomenon which is alive, beautiful and worthy of attention from us in academia. It should not be the preserve of one sector of the community. Good art such as this should be documented, so that those not in its immediate environment can access it too. This art is literature, much in the same way as any written work of art, and I shall employ some of the yardsticks used in analyzing "written" literature to this genre of "oral" literature. Indeed I will complement my sources with some songs and praise names that are in print.

Folklorists in the *folklore as tradition* school see folklore as *tradition*, that is, material handed down vertically, from an older, to a newer generation. Older folklorists have been characterized as "spiritual archaeologists" who try to reconstruct the tradition in its Ur form, and try to place it in time and space. The danger of regarding tradition as historically concluded is that it blocks the view of tradition as an emergent process. It is not a lively fossil which refuses to die. This, unfortunately, is the view held by many keepers of the oral tradition, who assert that what they produce is the same one handed down to them by earlier artists. We shall presently see that though the songs and epithets the griots of Dagbon sing have diachronic and synchronic dimensions, the creative genius, and virtuosity of the individual artist makes the difference between one's performance and others'. Modern folklore materials are now available in a multitude of forms, from oral, through written, to electronic modes. Drum music is primarily oral, but we now have *luŋa* music on compact discs and other digital and electronic media. They are also of interest in our present study.

Dundes in the preface to *International Folkloristics* says that the term 'folk' can refer to any group of people whatsoever who share at least one common factor and have some traditions it calls its own. A feeling of group identity is a key factor. In all societies, a part of the folklore is esoteric, and known only to specialists like shrine priests, fiddlers, or weather prophets. In Dagbon there are particular music and epithets that are specific to various professions. The butchers, blacksmiths, barbers, hunters, each have dance rhythm and praise names specific to them. This assigns a group identity to each. Some families also have family dances which are abbreviated praise names. All these have histories that can be expanded into long narratives that can be sung for the duration of a whole night. Examples of these are, *Naɣbiɛɣu* "awesome/ferocious cow", a name for Naa Abdulai (1849-1876) and his descendants, *naani goo* "trusted thorn", a name for Naa Andani and his family, *kuli noli* "a (good) watering hole", another name for Naa Abudu.

Epic narrations, praise singing sessions, and musical performances are held in space and time. There are shades of differences between these various performances, but they are essentially the same in character. Tradition as a process upholds and remodels ideas, verbal forms, attitudes, and norms. There is a relationship between the context and folklore, "the 'learning of the people', 'the wisdom of the people', the people's knowledge", as observed by Ben Amos (2000: 6). This knowledge is individually possessed by the drummers, who represent and re-present them to the best of their abilities. Nineteenth century national romanticism was suspicious of this process, because the feeling was that it could endanger tradition. The feeling then was that the olden days were better, and that the good bearers of tradition had died. Contrary to this belief that the re-presentation will endanger tradition, the process recreates tradition every time, and thus engenders it. Folklore is an integral part of culture and can be adapted to newer environments within which it finds itself. Folklore is thus transcultural or superorganic, and even when items of folklore travel into newer cultures we can still identify them as variants of the same type of phenomenon. The practice of praising royalty has a cultural function of elevating the institution of *nam* "royalty" to a near sacred status. It is akin to profaning the culture if a drummer does not acknowledge the presence of a royal when they meet, by properly clothing them with the appropriate family praise. The functional approach to folkloristics has been championed by the Anglo-Polish Malinowski (1946[1923]), Boas (2004) and Bascom (1953). We will analyze the praise epithets based on their functions. This will give us insights into culture, the whys, and the hows of cultural expressions.

THE DATA

My informants most times felt very uncomfortable divorcing the praise names I demanded from their song genres in which they are usually found. They needed to do their renditions with drum accompaniments. It is music that orders the raw materials used for creating the metaphor which the drummer-poets use in their art. Music is the essence of metaphor, the essence of music is feeling, not just sound, so that together they produce emotionally evocative messages. We need the four essential elements of music – rhythm, melody, harmony, and tone color – to bring up the complete spectacle. This corroborates Ben-Amos' assertion that folklore should not just be seen as collectible material, and that folklore in its cultural context happens as an "event" El Shamy (2004: ix) talks of folklore as a "process". The product cannot be separated from the process. They are in a continuum, the product arising in an artistic and creative communicative process. A compromise situation (a hybrid) had to be found by these informants, whereby they broke into song, as they tried to tell me praise names of chiefs. This was invariably done in a narrative format, where the chronological order in which chiefs came to power, as well as their praise epithets were narrated, and I was addressed as the target (a pseudo-patron) of the performance event. It is thus the process that brings out the best performances. What I did in eliciting these names out of context constituted a divorce of the praise epithets from their performance situations. This induced performance is regarded as sacrilegious by some of the drummers I came into contact with.

Kinney (1970), Chernoff (1979) and Locke (1990) have focused on music and rhythmic dimensions of the Dagomba drummers' craft; while DjeDje (2008) traces the history of the fiddle in Dagbon and West, focusing on the use of the Dagomba goonje in the service of their king. Agyekum (2002), Mahama (2004), and Yakubu (2005) have recently written short histories of the political struggles among the royals of Dagbon. My main interest is the linguistic and poetic aspects of the praises sung or chanted, and how rhythm may enhance this verbal component. This work is therefore an ethnopoetic one.

My MA thesis centered on the esthetic element in verbal communication in royal settings, but the present study is more interested in the subversive use to which oratory in general, and praise-singing or uttering in particular, can be put. Works of Obeng (1993), Yankah (1989, 1995), and Agyekum (1996) on various aspects of Akan verbal dueling, are useful for cross-linguistic comparison. Finnegan (1970) calls on African societies to document these oral repertories, which she sees as one form of literary expression with esthetic as well as practical appeal. These dimensions seem worth looking at, to me.

ETHNOGRAPHIC INQUIRY

The ethnographer describes the way of life of a particular people in as much detail as possible, with a view to revealing the nature of the culture. Like Thoms (1972), Boas (2004) and Glassie (1995), I do agree that material that will help us write about culture as an evolving way of life of a group, needs to be collected over a long period. This is the reason I have had to go back to this musical tradition over a period of three summers, and would have wished to stay there even longer. Much such ethnography has been documented by scholars in Africa and elsewhere. My work is an ethnographic inquiry into the genre of royal praise-naming, and the language that goes to the making of this lore. The language of these performances presents frames; the 'interpretive context providing guidelines for discriminating between orders of message' (see Bauman 1975: 292-3). This non-literal communication is intended to be interpreted as insinuations, jokes, imitatations, translations, or quotations.

At the start of my inquiry I relied on a participant observation line of inquiry at social events where griots acknowledge the presence of royal patrons by addressing them by their praise accolades. During my recent visit to the Tamale in the Gukpɛɣu traditional area, in the summer of 2007, I got into the acquaintance of a 'retired'[1] luŋa, who agreed to tutor me in the ways of the drummers. This shifted my methodology a bit, and he became my primary informant. Luŋa Alhassani took me through not only the praise epithets of Dagbaŋ nobles, but also the histories of these peoples and their towns and villages.

I also interviewed many praise singers to get to the core of their praise songs. Also, recorded songs by old and contemporary bards supplemented the field recordings I made. The superordinate position of the chief gives him a higher power over his subjects, so that he has a wider range of linguistic options than them. Those in positions of authority are more likely to have names that are highly proverbial, or potentially face-threatening to others. Interviewing these patrons gave me insight into how the praises really impact on them.

The use of proverbs is very popular among the Dagombas, who make use of both verse and witty prose statements to coin praise lines and accolades, which are also tagged "names". By entering into close and relatively long term contact with people in their everyday lives, the ethnographer becomes aware of and understands their beliefs and behavior more accurately (Hammersley 1992: 43). Ethnography should not just talk about cultures. It needs to accurately describe unfolding events. The researcher should be with and observe the community s/he is studying. This approach affords him/her access to local interpretative glosses of communicative material. Participating in and observing many performances, at funerals, coronations of chiefs and at other social occasions gave me insights into the goings on as they came up. As a native speaker of the language my intuitive knowledge of the culture has been an advantage, but this needs to be balanced with academic objectivity so as not to take anything for granted. Yankah (1987:15), in analyzing the dilemma of the native studying his people has this to say:

> Belonging to a culture does not necessarily make the researcher an insider to all constituents of the group he studies: . . . Where the researcher is not an integral part of such in-groups, he has to observe the normal protocol of penetration and learning.

---

[1] I call him "retired" because he has been in voluntary retirement for more than twenty years now, because he realized (possibly after soothsaying), that he would continue to have more enemies fighting him.

I actually saw that there was a wide variety of material that was so new to me that I needed to be literally schooled about it. Fieldwork is the practice of trying to understand others. It is a difficult, yet educating experience for the ethnographer. Fieldworkers are viewed between "marginal natives" to "professional strangers" (see Redfield 1955). Fieldwork asks the researcher to share first hand experiences s/he gathers. These must then be truthfully written down/ documented/ recorded. Whereas ethnography is the enterprise through which we get to the knowledge of a culture, it is the written or documented part that represents the culture. How representative is this 'skeleton'?

Relations of mine, who are from the drummer institution (*lunsi*), proved useful in this enterprise, and some shared some audio tapes with me that helped augment my primary data. These recordings from the Dagbon *baansi* (drummers/praise-singers) are an invaluable resource in my textual analysis. This will be material I can easily use to cross check some of the facts that were given to me by my primary informants. In order to appreciate the complexity of culture, an ethnographer must initially record events and conditions in as much detail as possible, so that the selection and search for patterns can come later. This has been my approach in undertaking the present study. Crane and Angrosino (1974) as say that the anthropologist's best interviews are often the result of chance encounters. This therefore means that no information can be dismissed outright without first having been closely scrutinized. These chance encounters came up interviews I had with people in my travels across Dagbon, which I had to quickly scribble down. Some library material will be consulted to complement what data I collected from the field.

Praise poetry here has the potential of inviting both intra and inter-group conflict. Which praise names are those that will engender good neighborliness, and which ones will unleash havoc on us? This, essentially, is what I intend to discuss in this book, with a view to setting a mechanism in motion that will encourage the positive use of praise poetry, and discourage those terms that are "conflict-inviting".

Of course, how closely, or deeply I can delve into this genre is dependent upon the rules laid down at the chief's palace[2], or by the taboo that surrounds the verbal process here, as for example, certain animal sacrifices may be needed at some points before certain bits of information may be divulged.

---

[2] The chief is the traditional leader in the area, and has to be consulted if one is to get any cooperation from any member of the chief's followers. Even present day government officials have to defer to him. He controls the praise- singers. They are functionally his wives.

Chapter 3

DRUM LORE IN DAGBON, AND PRAISE SINGING AS COMMUNICATION

The bachelor is inferior, the married man is superior. God is father to
both
He is father to both rich and poor. Father to the strong and the weak
He turns the Mighty into weaklings, and makes the weak Mighty
Whoever doubts this should look in front, and then, behind them,
up until they see their spine
Only then shall they perceive His wondrous Nature.[1]

COMMUNICATION

Drummers in Dagbon use their drum to communicate to and with their patrons. The drum is treated as an extension of the drummer. Whatever they say, sing, or play on their musical instrument is intended to affect the people in a certain way. All communication basically hinges upon an intention on the part of a sender to carry across a message to a hearer/receiver; see the various models of communication (e.g. Lasswell's (1949, 1960) linear, Shannon and Weaver's (1949) communications – engineering, and Newcomb's (1953) triangular.) This intention is then followed by a deliberate act on the initiator's part that makes them undertake a certain action, which is then sent across via a

---

[1] This is the first lesson in drumming given to the young drummer by his mentor. This in a way underscores the important, indeed sacred, position of the drummer in the Dagomba society as the entertainer, educator, and social commentator.

certain medium, to the receiver. Harold D. Lasswell (1949: 102) describes the
act of communication as one that answers the question,

Who
Says what
In which channel
To whom
With what effect

Sharon and Weaver's simple model of communication is also replicated
by John Lyons,[2] who describes it thus (see Figure 3.1):

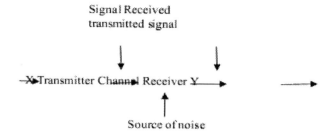

Figure 3.1. A model of communication.

What this figure essentially represents is that a signal is initiated by a
source, X, and transmitted via a channel, to a target audience, Y. In this dyadic
situation, there could be diversions, distortions, and other inhibitions, which
are perceived as 'noise'.

According to Lyons (1977:33) the sender, X, succeeds in making
"meaningful communication" happen when he makes "… the receiver aware
of something of which he was not previously aware." We shall see in our
discussions that the Dagomba praise-names-and-praise-singing genre, *salima*,
includes material which senders transmit to their audience that are not
necessarily novel. Their novelty may only be because they are just then being
instantiated by the present artist, and not that the material itself is newly
created. Successful communication occurs when the receiver appreciates a
message from a sender because they believe it was meant for them and not
another, and then act in a particular way in order to fulfill the sender's
communicative intention. When drummers sometimes press people with praise

---

[2] See John Lyons 1977:36.

names that are unknown to these patrons, or direct drum messages to them that the target audience cannot decode, it is usually difficult for the audience to disown these epithets. We find receivers 'paying' drummers even after the latter have misapplied praise epithets to the former in this manner, because it is the duty of a recipient of praises to reward the artist. It is a dishonor to not acknowledge the drummers' efforts. Some of the intended meanings can get lost this way, leading to some form of miscommunication. These elements that have the potential of diverting or distorting the message, referred to as 'semantic noise', include misunderstandings, taking words literally when a deeper meaning ought to be sought from what one hears, come up in the whole of drum-language and praise name communication scenarios. One also needs to have some contextual information, as with any specialized mode of communication, in order to decode some of the messages communicated. A lot of textual and intertextual references are utilized. Dagbon praise poetry is the preserve of the drummer-caste, which is the medium as well as the channel of communication of history, praise names and songs (more or less a kind of mass media). As observed by Lyons (38) some messages are "channel dependent". The Dagomba drummer and his principal instrument, the hour glass drum, are one and the same, and they have the same name: *luŋa*. The drum is an extension of the person, and what they jointly or singly communicate is culturally true. The drummer and the Dagomba royal are 'lovers'[3].

The drum 'talks' when it imitates the tonal patterns of the people[4]. There are specific drum beats that are synonymous with certain offices, and when drummed will signal that such persons are around, or are being alluded to. This moves to the realm of semiosis. This communicative function of folklore is shared by Ben Amos, Lomax and Abrahams who see folklore as a process that ties a performer and aesthetically marked material and audience together[5]. Jakobson (1960), like Peirce (1940), and Ogden and Richards (1923) before him, also espouses a semiotic model of communication, where an emotive force binds addresser and addressee in a perceiver/expresser interpersonal relationship. In the semiotic model the message comprises two parts, an

---

[3] The royal, whether male or female, has a masculine gender and the griot has a feminine gender (even though he is biologically a male).
[4] Dagbani is a tonal language, with 2 tones, high and low, which the drum mimics when it is made to 'talk'.
[5] See Dell Hymes 2000: 59, in Parédes, A. and Richard Bauman 2000.

expression (signifier) and a perception (signified)[6]. The sound the drum makes is not the same as the meaning, but they get associated to each other because the people have over the years decided to equate the sound to a specific meaning. The drum for example makes the sound *pam'pam'bi `li'* which has no independent meaning of its own, but has been used as a sign by the drummers to refer to the King of the Dagombas, the Yaa Naa, and cannot be drummed for any other.

MUSIC, PRAISE SINGING AND COMMUNICATION

Stone (2000) in her introduction to the Garland Handbook of African Music (GHAM) aptly captures the centrality of music in African life, the proliferation of ethnic groups across the continent notwithstanding. Music serves as the magnet that attracts all people to events, private and public, sacred or secular, royal or common; and also provides social commentary. For this reason, African music tends to be holistic, and brings together the three aspects of the theatre arts – music, drama, and dance. Each tune celebrates a certain element of the society: rites de passage, success, spurring members on to victory, praise-singing, or glorifying Mother Nature herself. These are all true for music in Dagbon, contemporary or old.

As a young city dweller I used to wonder what was interesting and worth listening to in what I considered "the rural folk's drum music." My father would sacrifice his night's sleep or attending the pre-Eid Muslim sermons to go and listen to some 'boring' tales told by an illiterate drummer during festivals. These were my myopic views of what the drummers produced as well as who they were. My idea of good music was shaped by my Western education and Westernized tastes, and further confused by views of what constituted good Islamic practice, which saw anything traditional as heathen. My earlier position was similar to that of the nineteenth century folklorists who classified folk songs using criteria that were extrinsic to the musical material itself, basing their classification on whether they thought particular songs fit into particular thematic categories, or could be used for certain motor functions. Twentieth century ethnomusicologists, according to Olivier and Riviere (2001: 480), paid attention to native classification discourse where the

---

[6] Perceiving the "sign" as comprising a signifier and the signified and the related language, langue and language in context, parole, were first introduced into the field by Ferdinand de Saussure.

social function and circumstances of organization were key foci. This, according to them, shifted the emphasis away from the music material. This suggests that music needs to be situated within a contextual frame, a kind of globule within which a musical performance may be analyzed or categorized. This latter category is where I stand at present, and would look at the drummers' praise epithets from a Dagbon political perspective rather than a contemporary Westernized Ghanaian's.

One of the basic characteristics of African music, and indeed music in general, is that it is a metaphor of life, and mirrors the goings on in the society; a kind of 'Little Community', through whose eyes the larger society's worldview is encapsulated. Redfield (1955) and Geertz (1973) search for clarity and understanding of the methods by which the ways of small communities can be described, with the ultimate goal of linking the little community's report to that of the larger community, re-echoing the part-whole schema. As cultural commentators and historians, Dagomba *lunsi*[7] pursue a means of livelihood by drumming at functions and being rewarded by patrons; and also act as tradition bearers in their keeping of the oral histories of the ethnic group. Their craft is thus both an economic endeavor and a cultural responsibility over the years. These two roles can be broadly seen as synchronic and diachronic, respectively. While their art meets their current economic needs, the drummers, in keeping us abreast of what went by in previous epochs, serve as living archives and the collective memory of the populace. Where would we then place contemporary folk musicians? *Luntali*, the craft of the *lunsi*, is a casted institution, but one does not have to belong to this caste to be a pop musician, as practiced in contemporary times. The drummer is a tradition bearer, who blends theory and practice in his performance. He has the "book of rules" in his possession, one written by the ancestors which he interprets, and then also watches for feedback from everyone. Their role as social commentators is complemented by the new pop musician, who is also referred to as a *baanga* 'singer', but cannot engage in the traditional praise singing, *salima*.

Names that shall be analyzed in this book are divided into *personal*, *lineage* and *town name praise* epithets. We find drummers (*lunsi*), royals who do not yet have towns or villages to rule (*nabi'yɔnsi*), as well as prominent commoners (*tarimba*), taking praise names. These names are of the types that

---

[7] Their role is akin to that of the Mandinka jeli, the Wolof gewel, the Fulbe gawlo, all of whom were bardic traditions that had contact with the royals of ancient Ghana and Mali empires.

mock or ridicule others (*ansarisi*), nicknames (*yu'pirisi/yu'parisi*), or town/village praise names (*tinsi yuya*). Some names, given to children born under mysterious conditions by their parents, are proverbial, e.g. Timtituvuri "dregs of the medicine", Yenzoo "wisdom is rife", Kpaɣnimbu/Kpuɣnimbu "you have taken (married) a wondrous being".

I shall do a textual analysis of the epithets that I have collected. Of what are they composed? What images are portrayed in these texts? The epithets make use of many animal characters. What similarities or differences exist between the animals used in juxtaposition or opposition to each other? What does each animal symbolize, and how do they compare with the personalities they refer to in real life? Dagomba animal tales are metaphors of life itself. The individual, like the animal in a text (verbal or written), is in a complex web of relationships. As is the case with many African societies, the self is always linked to society, even though in recent times there are moves by many to hold themselves outside the dominance of the society. Folktales as common cultural property espouse the general worldview. Changing times however, bring with them modifications in the way contemporary society views modern phenomena. According to Rattray (1928: 9) the choice of the animals that impersonate human personages is not done haphazardly. "They were chosen with all the cleverness and insight into their various characteristics." That is the reason hyena as a character in Dagomba folktales is a villain, for he is so individualistic and self-centered that he seeks no one's assistance. He trusts his strength and wile to see him through, plus he does not want to share his spoils with others, hence his not engaging in joint enterprises. The spider is always weaving a net (trap) to capture or ensnare his prey. This trait is likened to that of a trickster who is always scheming to dupe or outwit his victims. Other animals and traits associated with them include, Cat: secrecy/ thoughtfulness; Buffalo: brute strength; Ant: industry/team spiritedness; Spider: greed; Billy-Goat: wisdom/lechery; Lion: royalty[8] (see El-Shamy (2005) for an exposé of similar motifs.) Animals play as much a key role in the world of folktales as they do in praise naming and epic poetry; but it takes a specialist to properly use the animal idiom in praise-names or epics. These specialists are the drummer-poet-raconteur.

The hierarchy of people in the Dagbon kingdom is like that in the in the animal kingdom, where the Lion is lord. The symbol of the highest traditional leader of Dagbamba, the *Yaa Naa*, is the lion. He is metonymically "The *Lion*

---

[8] See list of some animals used in the praise epithets, in Appendix 7.

of Dagbon". In the language of poetry Dagbon is also referred to as "Yɔɣu", the same term used to refer to the Wild/forest. So, the Yaa Naa is to Dagbon what the Lion is to the Forest. Lawuyi (1990: 74) observes the same phenomenon among the Yoruba of Southern Nigeria where stories involving the Lion often have him sit in court and arbitrate between litigating animals.

What does the aggregate of these epithets tell us about the people's worldview? Dramatis personae found in many of the praise names are presented in ways that mirror the people's way of perceiving the world. Many names will draw on the Dagomba belief in virtue being better than wealth, reincarnation of ancestors, belief in magic, polygamy, truth's ultimate victory over falsehood, and family integrity. Malinowski (1922: 517) says it is the native's ". . . outlook on things, his *Weltanschauung*", that motivates him to study the world around them. Folktales, the epic narratives, and the praise names and histories that surround the praise names, no doubt provide an avenue for Dagombas to look out upon their universe. In this scheme of things the stories told in Dagbon tie the self, others, and universe together in their telling. Their experiences merge, that is, there is a shared experience, which allows the human audience to identify with or conceptualize the events unfolding in the narratives. The Dagbon cosmos generally centers on geographic areas within the ethnic group's land borders. Foster (1966) equates worldview to cosmology, and this fades to values (see Dundes 2000). So, what does the Dagomba praise name tell us about the people's notion of the universe and what the people's values are? We shall see this in the chapters that follow.

THE DRUMMER

Every culture is a precipitate of its history. Until very recently[9], the history of the Dagbon nation has largely been kept by the drummers, who narrate it at epic singing sessions during festivals. If the importance of history cannot be overemphasized, it goes without saying that the luŋa is very vital to the survival of Dagbon's culture. European history, for example, has been documented for centuries, but only a little part of Dagbon's history has been documented, and this has been largely after the mid twentieth century.

---

[9] A. W. Cardinal 1931:230-279, Fage 1964, and Martin Staniland 1975 have been the few authors to have done some in-depth study into the stories of the Kings of Dagbon.

Many a drummer has aptly defined their roles in performance, as reported by Belcher (1999: 8) who quotes the griot Mamadou Kouaté, from Djibril Tamsir's Niane's *Soundiata*,

> ... we are vessels of speech, we are the repositories which harbour secrets many centuries old. The art of eloquence has no secrets for us; without Us the names of kings would vanish into oblivion, we are the memory of mankind; by the spoken word we bring to bring to life the deeds and exploits of kings for younger generations.

Similarly, at an evening of epic poetry the luŋa Issah Zɔhi of Yendi said,

> We speak of events that have come to pass.
> The fact is an event that has not occurred we do not even know it.
> My father has asked that I publicize what the world hides.
> My father told me that if a thing happens once, I should announce
> it ten times; there is no problem about that.
> But what has not happened, I should never say it has.

They, the drummers, also say it is for the benefit of those not present today, that the griot institution was put in place by our forebears. Many see the Dagomba drummer primarily as an entertainer. The artistic function is important, not as an end in itself but as a means to achieving a higher end, which is the transmission of historical and cultural information. As observed by Titon (2005: 13) this emotive force evoked by the drummers' music carries us to more serious realms.

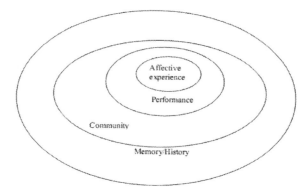

Figure 3.2. Titon's Music-Culture model.

At the center of the music (as you experience it) is its

> radiating power, its emotional impact – assent, smile,
> nod your head, sway your shoulders, dance. That is called
> music's affect, its power to move, and which forms the
> center of the model.

Titon (1998:11) uses the following model to represent his music-culture model, in which music as an affective experience binds performers and audiences in time and space:

This scheme moves from performers to performance, which is part of the flow of the community's everyday life. In the recitation of the epic story of Naa Andani Girilɔŋ, also known as *Naani Goo* (reigned 1876-1899), "the trusted thorn" for example, the music makes

people dance to its rhythm while the lyrics simultaneously warn them to be wary of false friends and kin. Andani as a non-titled youth goes to fight to rescue his brother Naa Abdulai Naɣbiɛɣu from the Baasari[10]. He is accompanied by kith and kin to Baasari land, but they all desert him when it is time to do battle, so that should he perish they would have a better chance of ascending to the throne. This performance takes its material from the community's collective memory and history.

Oppong (1973:13) likewise observes that the drum histories of the Dagombas have preserved rich historical narratives. These narratives have recently been shown to be founded upon facts in several respects by archaeological, linguistic and written data. Oral tradition has it that the founders of the Mole-Dagbani ethnic groups came from the east of Lake Chad towards the end of the fifteenth century to settle in their present northern part of Ghana, having defeated existing ethnic groups - Vagala, Sisaala, Tampilinsi - and imposing their authority over them. Staniland (1975:3) says that the Mole-Dagbani people emigrated from Zamfara, located to the north of Borgu in Northern Nigeria around the thirteenth century. Staniland (ibid) quotes Fage (1964) as saying the Dagomba were part of a movement which also created the Mamprusi, Nanumba, and Mossi states.

Dagombas of the recent past have mostly been subsistence farmers who produced yam, maize, millet, sorghum and rice. This is still the practice among rural folk. The land lies in the savannah woodland and has trees of economic

---

[10] The Baasari is a neighboring ethnic group akin to the Konkomba, and found to the east of Dagbon, on the Ghana-Togo border.

value, such as the *taanga* "shea tree", *doo* "Dawadawa (a local soup seasoning)", *tua* "Baobab", *guŋa* "silk cotton (Kapok) and Mangoes (newly introduced). These trees were usually not cut even when the land is prepared for farming or building construction. They provide fruits, oil, shade and are of medicinal value. Recent global economics is however changing this trend, and large tracts of these age-old economic trees are cut down and replaced with plantations of mangoes for export to Western markets. Each family keeps livestock - chickens, guinea fowls, turkey, goats and cattle. The fowls and goats are used for sacrifice and for sale. Guinea fowls are slaughtered to welcome visitors, he-goats are also killed to grace festive occasions. Cattle and rams may be slaughtered at important funerals. Cattle are a prized lot, with each family (*daŋ*) owning its cattle. Cattle from the family kraal are sold to settle family problems, and acquire wives, or they are slaughtered at family funerals. The family cattle are held in trust by the *dɔɣirikpɛma* 'family head'. These are the basic ingredients that go into the making of praise epithets and for these reasons we find many of the praise names revolving around these cultural practices mentioned above.

Professional skills include those of the *wanzam* (or *gunu*), 'barber', *luŋa* 'drummer', *goonje* 'fiddler', *machele* 'blacksmith', *baɣa* 'soothsayer' the *nakɔha* 'butcher' and the *kasiɣira* 'undertaker'. From about the beginning of the eighteenth century the *afa* 'Muslim cleric' has played so significant a role that this has become a professional career just like any of those mentioned above (see Lubeck (1968)) for how the Hausa's assimilated into Dagbon). These trades often entail a long period of apprenticeship with an elder craftsman, and often are the preserves of an exclusive kin group. Other jobs, which do not usually entail such long periods of training, include those of the *shɛ'shɛra* 'a local tailor', and the *gbanzaba* 'cobbler'. These jobs are mainly masculine ones. Women also engage in *yaɣ'mebo* 'pottery', *kpa'tabo* 'sheabutter processing', *kulikuli malibu* 'groundnut (peanut) oil extraction, *daa'biligu* 'petty trading (usually of cooked foods)', *kpaligu tambu* 'dawadawa making', and *gum'mibu* 'spinning cotton thread'. Some of these serve to generate income for the purchase of their needs. These professions are echoed in the prelude to epic performances, see Appendix 5, where the artist mentions cotton processing, hunting, farming, wood-carving, and of course, drumming.

THE PLACE OF THE DRUMMER IN THE SOCIETY

One of my informants remarked that, "without the drummer there is no *nam* 'royalty', and without royalty there is no group." In essence what he was telling me was that without the drummer there can be no group identity. Multilingual Ghana (which has about sixty languages) is like a market place, where each person should look out for kith and kin. The drummer is the one to remind us of where we are coming from, and also show us the way forward. A praise epithet of Naa Andani Naasakai describes the dilemma of the detribalized, as one who has left his kin for wealthy strangers. He will be the biggest loser. In his words,

> Jɛri' zaa kpe daa n ti zaɣisi o yiŋnim dɔlibu ka chɛn dɔli kaanila bundaamba.
> Daa yi yi o ni kuli o ko.
> The fool has neglected family and opted to follow wealthy strangers.
> When he is abandoned he will be the ultimate loser.

There are so many similarities between the bardic traditions of Dagbon and those from the Mandinka of Mali, Senegal, Gambia, and the Sahelian region, that these suggest a common origin. Descriptions of various functions performed by the jeli of Mali, Gambia and Senegal fit those performed by the Dagomba luŋa aptly. Innes (1976: 5) quoted in Locke (2005: 95) describes the relationship between the kings and the *jeli/jali* as a beneficial one,

> Griots woke the king each morning by singing his praises outside
> his quarters, they accompanied him wherever he traveled, singing
> and playing behind him and especially when he met another king,
> they were in attendance singing their patrons praises. From time to
> time a court griot would entertain the king and members of his court
> by reciting accounts of the careers of some of the king's forebears,
> perhaps of some deeds of the king himself ... The whole narration
> glorified the king, often bathing him in the reflected glory of his
> mighty ancestors ... [The griot] would take real pride in [this] history
> and would want to present it in the best possible light, for he would
> surely feel able to share in the glory of his patron's family.

Locke's (2005:99) summarises the lunsi's role as,

> Lunsi each act as speech artist, family historian, royal   advisor, cultural
> specialist, and entertainer.

We shall return to a more detailed discussion of this symbiotic relation when we turn to look at the praise singing sessions and their analyses, especially where the ancestors of griots perished in battles beside their patrons' forebears.

Irvine (1989: 253) observes that among rural Wolof of Senegal, there is a series of ranked, endogamous occupational groups, called "castes" in the ethnographic literature on the region. She says that caste differences are culturally associated with differences in speech style. A style connected with high rank (*waxu geer*, "noble speech") contrasts with a style connected with low rank (*waxu gewel*, "griot speech," so named after the bardic caste which in some respects is said to epitomize low-ranking groups). But, unlike the Wolof *gewel*, Dagomba lunsi are not low-ranking: they actually once belonged to the royal hierarchy but got eliminated into the commoner class as contests for ascendancy to the Yani skin grew keener with more eligible princes being born to the Kings. There is a hierarchy of prestigious titles within the drummer caste, which makes them chiefs in their own right. The drummer is beloved of the ruler, and each addresses the other in terms of endearment, the chief being the husband and the drummer his wife[11]. A drummer's marketability depends not only upon his ability to play the drum, flute or fiddle, but more on his verbal skills. This constitutes a major economic resource which will eventually give a young drummer an important position in life. Good singers will normally get better material rewards than average or mediocre ones. This indexical correlation between drummers' linguistic and material goods is the focus of Irvine's study of the Wolof gewel. Unlike their *waxu gewel* 'cousins' the *lunsi's* speech can be described as noble and can be refined even if the speech content is profane. Drummers/griots are indispensable in traditional discourse management. Royals rely on them to pick apt praise epithets, because their traditional profession employs a lot of rhetoric. They are eloquent and noted to be able to speak the unspeakable word and profanities if they have to.

Their counterpart the gewel is noted by Irvine (1989: 257) to be,

> persuasive [in] speechmaking on a patron's behalf, making
> entertaining conversation, transmitting messages to the public,
> and performing the various genres of praise-singing. Not everyone
> who might be born with the appropriate raw talent can become a
> professional bard-for that one must be born into the griot caste.
> But within that category, the most talented and skillful
> griots earn high rewards and are sought after by would-be patrons,
> such as village-level political leaders (or those who seek leadership

---

[11] Kwesi Yankah 1995 observes the same type of relationship between the Asante king and his praise singer.

positions). High-ranking political leaders do not engage in these
griot-linked forms of discourse themselves; to do so would be
incompatible with their "nobility" and qualifications for office.
But their ability to recruit and pay a skillful, reputable griot to
speak on their behalf is essential, both to hold high position
and to gain access to it in the first place.

This underscores the griot's important role as a teacher, negotiator, coach, entertainer, and tradition bearer. He is materially rewarded because he is the keeper of the sacred word, that is the ethnic group's history, and but for him there would be no group identity so to speak. So sacred are their words that, a fowl or a ram has to be sacrificed to the ancestral spirits before detailed narrations are made. My informant sacrificed a white chicken before delving into the deeper secrets of his craft. Johnson (1992: 3) observes the same phenomenon among the Mande, that:

> ... the power of their speech is considered more than merely
> entertaining or persuasive. It is common belief that the power of the
> occult is conveyed in the bard's words...

It was this pedagogical role my principal informant played when he schooled me in the art of royal onomastics, see photograph below,

Figure 3.3. Author being instructed by drummer.

Without the drummer there is no music to grace festive occasions. They play the important role of providing music for the dancing populace.

Figure 3.4. Drummers provide music at social events.

TRAINING OF A TRADITION BEARER

Political and Ethnographic History

The chief, like the chieftaincy institution, synecdochically represents the entire community. He is the axis of political relations, and symbolises the integrity and value-system of the ethnic group. Oppong (1973) in describing the chief says he is the ruler and representative of his people. He is

> . . . the receiver and distributor of tribute; the patron of craftsmen, musicians and followers; the main arbitrator in disputes and quarrels; the hub of the communication system and the collector and distributor of news. He is also the main locus of power in the community . . . (and) he possesses medicines, tim (which) includes powers from his ancestors.

Religious belief in Dagbon hinges on belief in the *Naawuni* 'the Supreme Being', *buɣa* 'nature spirits', *tiŋgbana* 'lesser earth spirits', and *yaannima/kpiimba* 'spirits of the dead/ancestral spirits'. The chief is an incarnation of the gods and ancestral spirits, and as such is accorded the utmost reverence. The ruler is both *andunia naawuni* 'earth's god' and *buɣa siɣilana* "reincarnate of the ancestral shrines". This reflects in all spheres of the people's lives, so that whoever wishes to prosper would do well not to incur the wrath of these deities or their representative.

Dagbon contains a number of hierarchically stratified chiefdoms which are patrilineally inherited. As previously stated, the kingdom evolved out of conquest with an invading ruling class imposing itself over the indigenes that became the commoner estate (*dagban-dabba* or *tarimba*). Today only the elders and some chiefdoms (e.g., Katariga, Tamale Dakpema and Kakpaɣiyili) are held by descendants of the earth priests (*tindaamba (tindana* SG*)*).

Political power (*nam*) is now the preserve of the invader class. In Dagbaŋ the Yaa Naa (literally means 'King of Power') owns the land, and may delegate a portion to divisional and village chiefs. He, in consultation with his ancestors (through divination) and elders confers political office to royals based upon legitimate agnatic descent; so that sometimes sons or daughters of important chiefs may be able to succeed their mothers' brothers. In the recent past the Yaa Naa was the "sovereign", and "Commander-In-Chief of the Dagbon Military Establishment" (see Mahama 2004: iii). Rattray (1932:567) observes that the king also rewards his loyal officials or war captains with chiefdoms that can be held by non-royal officials (e.g., Tolon was given to the Yaa Naa's *Kpanalana* `spear bearer').

According to oral tradition there have been forty Yaa Naas since the founding of the Dagbon state. These include chiefs from Naa Shitɔbu through to the current Yaa Naa, Yakubu Andani II, who has reigned since 1974[12]. In the royal genealogy the office of Yaa Naa is restricted to the senior sons of senior sons, and those of royal descent whose fathers did not become chiefs became commoners. This was what happened to Bizuŋ and his descendants.

Prussin (1969), Oppong (1973) and Staniland (1975) observe that the physical structure of the village community is that of closely grouped circular compounds, the chief's domed reception hall being the most prominent. The village is divided into wards or quarters (*fɔna,* SING. *fɔŋ*), each ward being identified with the head or by the specialist group that dominates it, e.g., *nayili fɔŋ* "the chief's quarter", *nakɔhigu fɔŋ* "the butchers' quarter", etc). The

---

[12] He was murdered on March 27, 2002, but his funeral has not yet been observed. His regent is acting King.

warriors' quarter is usually behind the chief's so that they are on hand to defend their patron as and when the need arises. The warriors, who trace their origin from Ashanti, still use Akan names, even through corrupted forms (e.g., Chinto, Kɔbana, Kofi, Dua, Champɔŋ, Achiri, and Achina), and sit on stools or chairs like their Ashanti ancestors rather than on skins.

The drummer is strategically placed in the midst of this political environment, and everyone has need for his services. He is the most important of the principal communicative officials of the chief. There cannot be a royal house where there is no drummer. Salifu (2007: 99) notes that,

> By and large, communicating with the chief involves a
> process of surrogation either through a musical instrument
> (drum, fiddle or flute) or an elder . . . [and] some messages
> can only be passed on to the Yaa Naa by way of drumming.

If these special messages must be relayed via the drum it means the drummer has to be there when needed to perform this function.

DjeDje (2008: 188) quotes Chernoff (1997: 102) that,

> A sense of history is central to the integration of Dagbamba culture and to the Dagbamba musical heritage . . . A Dagomba drummer is a political figure whose influence extends
>
> from conferring varying degrees of respect on rulers, to discriminating the status of individual lineage identities at social gatherings. As such drummers acquire high respect not only for their historical erudition but for their detailed knowledge of the   kinship patterns of their local communities.

This high status reflects in the physical proximity of the *namo naa* "chief drummer" to the king. Of all the elders and court officials at the palace of the Yaa Naa he is the only one who has a permanent shed (*sampaa*) situated in the royal compound. He places higher than the king's security apparatus, whose presence is at the rear of the chief's house. This public record keeper is present when the "king" is born, and there to announce his death when it occurs, see Iddi (1968: 6). Historically, the great ancestor of all drummers, Bizuŋ, son of Naa Nyaɣsi, was apprenticed to Lun' ʒaɣu to be schooled in the art of drumming and praise singing. With time he became the stellar drummer. Drummers do not ascend to the high office of Yaa Naa as their great ancestor,

Nyaɣ si once did. His orphaned son Bizuŋ [13](literally means "stranger-child") had to scrounge for food from other children because he had lost his mother early in childhood. He resorted to drumming on a broken gourd with a stick when he was hungry. The young motherless player's music attracted the attention he needed, which often led to one of the more fortunate children giving him a piece to eat. Upon hearing of his young son Bizuŋ's aptitude for music Naa Nyaɣ si apprentices him to the master drummer, Lun' ʒ aɣ u, to help nurture his talent.

Training

As previously mentioned, lunsi are held in high esteem by the whole populace. Training of a luŋa starts in early childhood, (see figure 3.5 below). One is nominally a luŋa by virtue of being born into the drummer caste, and starts receiving instructions immediately after they have been weaned from the mother. It is the general practice to give out a biological son to a colleague drummer to teach the art of drumming. It is a life-long profession and thus needs to be taken very seriously. Adult drummers may farm or engage in other jobs, but they are primarily drummers.

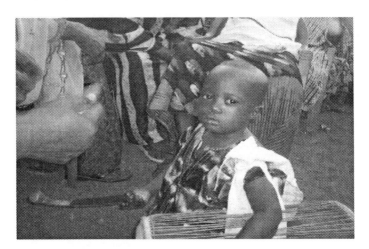

Figure 3.5. Young drummer at a social event.

---

[13] Invoking the spirit of Bizuŋ before a performance is akin to invoking the Muse. That is the spirit of the drum. They will also swear by their ancestor Bizuŋ and his drum-stick to indicate the veracity of what they say.

Like Bizuŋ, when children are apprenticed to seasoned drummers who become their 'drum-fathers', they (the neophytes) sometimes move to reside with their tutors and are raised as their own. The children are required to help with work on the farm as well as undertake domestic chores around the house. This same manner of training is found among the jeli of The Gambia and Mali

Instruction in drumming begins with the young child observing adult drummers at social occasions like funerals and coronation ceremonies; and listening to the father narrate the political life histories accompanied by the praise names of the royals, which more or less equates to the history of the ethnic group. After supper the drum father would instruct the trainee drummer in the history of the royal families, and from time to time test the pupil's retention of what has been taught him by making him recite particular texts to his (the teacher's) hearing. Strict sanctions are applied when students fail to deliver. Corporal punishment is a common punishment for those who are slow at memorizing their teachers' lessons. The student drummer practices his lessons on market days by drumming the stock phrase *dakɔli n nyɛ bia* "the bachelor is inferior" at the market. By way of encouragement he is given monetary presents by traders who would also occasionally ask him to eulogize their forebears. He thus puts what he was taught into practice.

After a period of training, the young drummer is allowed to play in the ensemble in an answering role. There is usually a master drummer (*lun' dɔɣu* literally, 'male drum') who sets the pace as well as gives the rhythm in a call-and-response situation, and a team of drummers who give a chorus drum-response. When he is deemed to have mastered play enough he can then be allowed to play the bass drum (*gungɔŋ*), and later on could be assigned an assistant master drummer status whereby he responds to a master drummer's signal and then cues the other members of the ensemble. Any money got from an outing is brought home to the head drummer who distributes it among all the drummers. It is ominous to hide any such money from the group. The instructional content is esoteric and considered sacred, so magical charms and potions are sought to enhance the learner's prowess and retentive memory, and also ward off the evil-eye of rivals and envious people.

What the drummer essentially stands for, and demonstrates in his duty is that he is a tool used by the ethnic group to delineate who they are, and if you as an individual recognize that you belong to this group you must respect them as the tradition bearers. They do not beg you for your money or attention. Any *Dagbaŋ bilichina* 'conscientious Dagomba citizen' ought to see it as his/her duty to see to the drummers' upkeep just as they (the drummers) have sacrificed over centuries to keep the oral tradition alive by reminding us of our individual and the collective histories. They at the same time punctuate our everyday life with their music and counsel, and also encourage us to strive for a better tomorrow.

El-Shamy (1967)'s discussion of 'cues' in his book fits the role the drummers of Dagbon play. In their role as the watchman of Dagomba society drummers cue their patrons as well as secondary audiences. Cues according to him, are stimuli that control the patron's social behavior according to the norms and values of his culture, and a failure to recognize these cues (secondary stimuli forces) will result in improper or inadequate behavior, leading to punishment for deviation, (El-Shamy 1967: 68). On the role of the performer, Bauman (2007: 36) says they are both admired and feared, ". . . admired for their artistic skill and power for the enhancement of experience they provide, feared because of the potential they represent for subverting and transforming the status quo."

Memorization plays a very important role in the reproduction of story lines for historical narratives and epics. Drummers however, need not memorize a whole song verbatim. What they must not forget, and need to retain, are the specific praise epithets of individuals, names these personages identify as theirs, or belonging to their family lineage. If bards forget those ones then they have lost their major stock in trade. Griots need to recall patrons' epithets they learnt previously, and then spice these stock, proverbial, or witty phrases with their poetic acumen to suit current performance situations. It is this recall, according to El-Shamy (1967:137) that,

> results in remembering, if the material was retained , or in the
> inability to remember, if the material was forgotten, suppressed
> or inhibited . . . [and a drummer's] efforts could result in remembering
> the item fully (if he retained all the details), in remembering only a
> fragment, or failure to remember any of the details.

The drummer in the light of these last statements, cherishes the power to have a good retentive memory, and will go to any length to improve his capacity to delve deep into his mental faculties to retrieve his material. Drummers believe in potions that will boost their memory, and lick concoctions for memory, known as *teeli* "Memory" before they go out to perform. They cry out to the spirits of memory and oratory when they faulter during performance.

Chapter 4

MUSIC, EDUCATION, HISTORY, AND POESY AS FUNCTIONS OF DRUMMERS

> One line of a drummer's praise is better than
> A hundred pilgrimages to Mecca.
> (Source: an aspirant to royal title.)

In this chapter I argue that the verbal sign (a praise name) relates to a political economy (Dagbon) in many ways: by denoting it; by indexing parts of it; by depicting it as part of a larger discourse (both diachronic and synchronic) that has the potential to change emotions, for better or worse. The musician-historian corps of the chief's court includes the hour-glass drummers (*lunsi*), the fiddlers (*goonjenima* SG *goonje*), the twin-talking drum players (*akarimanima* SG *akarima*) and the horn/flute blowers (*yu' piɛbiriba* SG *yu' piɛbira*). Any of these can sing praises and are subsumed under the cover term *luŋa* 'drummer'. They are collectively referred to as *baansi* (*baanga* SG) 'singers/bards'. This craft of the *baansi* is a 'course' in music, communication, pedagogy, political economy, history and literature. Praise names encode these aspects of the life of Dagbamba. A study of *salima* will eventually lead to a lesson in these cultural elements.

Dagombas see cultivated speech as comprising language that utilises embellished speech. Common everyday discourse is so pregnant with parables and allegories that a person's cultivation is indicated by the elegance of his/her imagery and facility in drawing upon the expansive store of proverbs to illustrate his/her points. A royal setting requires an even more elegant register than would be used in ordinary settings. Like most Africans (see Chernoff 1979:161) Dagombas "pay a great deal of attention to social formalities, to etiquette, to status differences, and to institutional procedures and roles because these conventions stand as the foundation of their community life, providing a framework to help them know what is happening and to get into it." A notable proverb says that,

> Nir' zinli n nyɛ dariga ka bɛ mali li n siviri o puuni n ti nyari o puuni yɛla. A person's tongue constitutes the ladder via which we descend into their internal parts to find out what they are made up of.

This attests to the fact that the tongue is indeed a very powerful tool in man's social life; and by extension, it underscores the power of the spoken word. A carrier/bringer of good news, and one who has a cultivated speech both have 'sweet-tongue-water', in Dagbani, *o zilin kom nyaɣisa/viɛla* 'the water from his/her tongue is sweet/beautiful', and a singer with a mellifluous voice is described as one whose voice is sweet, *o kukɔli nyaɣisa*. One who lacks proper verbal skills is likened to a deaf-mute.

A person with a savoir faire is one who among other things, has the ability to keep secrets, carry messages across accurately, and not be a gossip. While possessing an incisive tongue is not one of the attributes one will be liked for, it could come in handy when drummers use it to curtail excesses among royals and higher ups in society. In Dagbon, it is the person's facility to use language that primarily gives an indication of who s/he is.

MUSIC, DIALOGUE AND COMMUNICATION

The drummer is the primary musician of Dagbon. He provides music for all social functions: naming ceremonies, weddings, outdooring of newly enskinned[1] chiefs, during final funeral rites, and at festivals. They also provide solemn music when aged persons or important personalities are recently deceased, and yet to be buried. In everyday drumming, Dagomba drum music employs a call and response format, where a *lun' dɔɣu* 'male/lead drums' sets the pace and the ensemble responds to his calls. This lead drum also improvises as well as decides when to change tunes. Drummers may choose to

---

[1] The term "enskinned" is to the Dagomba what 'enthroned' is to the English. Dagomba Kings/chiefs sit on animal skins placed on platforms, and are enskinned when invested with kingly powers. The Yaa Naa sits on lion skins, but village chiefs sit on cow skins.

give instrumental renditions of music and praises, or drum with vocal accompaniment or vocal music alone. But, when they produce music they intend that it be interpreted beyond the entertainment value derived. Each drummed text is surrounded by a lot of history, which needs to be combined in order to get a holistic theatrical experience. The meaning of a text is negotiated between speaker/ producer, and the audience/ consumer and their shared history. This view has been noted elsewhere by Volosinov (1973: 103), and Bakhtin (1986: 99). Texts relate to other texts, so that, even the most homogeneous self-contained texts exhibit elements that link it to texts, with different contexts, different norms, and different voices. Bauman (2004) calls this intertextuality.

In requesting a particular tune to be played for one to dance[2], a particular message is communicated between requestor, musician and spectators, who see the particular tune as iconic, in that it links the requestor to a particular person in history who is identified as the originator of the song. The choice is also an unspoken sign of who its requestor is or wants to be identified with. This semiotic potential of music is captured by Turino (1999: 236) when he says that,

> Music integrates the affective and identity-forming potentials
> of both icons and indices in special ways, and is thus a central
> resource in events and propaganda aimed at creating social unity,
> participation, and purpose.

The iconic dance tunes (e.g., *naani goo*, and *naɣ' biɛɣu*) chosen will thus indicate whether one wants to be identified as belonging to, for example, the Andani lineage or an Abudu one respectively. This same resource that creates social unity has a divisive potential in Dagbon, and has polarized the citizenry into these two antagonistic clans. If a known Abudu descendant chooses to dance to *naani goo* rather than the usual *naɣ' biɛɣu* he is associated with, he sends a message of wanting to accommodate in with his Andani cousins.

In the opening quote I use the words attributed to a chief of Savilugu, Yoo naa Abdulai Gurigurilo, which alludes to the emotive force the music of drummers carry. This is more appreciated than the ultimate goal of a Muslim (fulfilling the fifth pillar of Islam, which is, performing the Hajj to the Holy land, Mecca). The term al-Hajj is very prestigious in Dagbon, but this does not

---

[2] There are two broad "dance" categories, the mundane and the ritualistic. Ritual dances are serious moments and are not to be interpreted as mere entertainment.

measure up to being the target of the music of praise poetry from a *luŋa*. *Luŋa* music marks a person's identity, not just as a Dagbana, but as a *Dagban nabia* (a royal Dagomba). Praising royalty tends to be dialogic, and involves an interchange with the subject while others observe. Like Yoruba *oriki* Dagbon *salima* addresses the subject, but also requires a third party audience to listen, because they are part of, and share common identity with the patron. The drummer would occasionally resort to addressing an observing bystander, who now becomes part of his immediate audience and telling him '*o yaba n daa yɛli ni --- ka a mi yaba yɛli ni ---*' 'X's grandfather said that --- and your grandfather too said ---' drawing in the third party to not just be passive, but to be one who would share part of the glory as well as authenticate the on-going discourse. The audience eventually becomes one family with a common identity, for praise singers will try to show linkages in family trees of primary and secondary audiences. Patrons who feel they have been wrongly allied to families draw the performers' attention to the anomaly and ask for corrections to be made.

EDUCATION AND HISTORY

Before the arrival of western formal education in Dagbon at the turn of the twentieth century, children had the bulk of their education via "informal" means: observing the ways of adults, through folktales, proverb lore, personal narratives from older family members, especially about 'the good old days'. Drummers, as keepers of the oral tradition, were both instructors in etiquette and practitioners of performative arts. When the drummers recount Naa Dariʒiɛɣu's (reigned 1543-1554) history and his praises they also remind all princes, and by extension the whole populace, to be generous to the drummer at all times because drummers stand by their patrons through thick and thin. One who ignores the needs of the drummer will be an ingrate, for the drummers have since ancestral times stood by and served the kings, their 'husbands', and it is their turn to be extended a helping hand. Luŋa Alhassan uses Naa Dariʒiɛɣu's story to illustrate this, saying that,

> O daa nyɛla Kɔliŋ paɣisara viɛlim ka kpalim Kɔlinsi ni. Tɔlana bia yi diri nam ŋun dimi ka mi bɛ nyaaŋa yɛla, dama namo naa Bizuŋ bia mini o lun' doli daa doli o mi ti kpalim Kɔliŋ.

He saw the beauty of Gonja women and remained among the Gonjas. When a King reins he should remember he has followers who stick with him through thick and thin like the head drummer and his drum-stick who followed him (into battle) and fell there.

In this excerpt which encodes a lot of history, Naa Dariʒiɛʏu, son of Naa Zɔŋ and of a Gonja mother, was raised by his maternal uncle. It was when he came of age that he returned to Dagbon to become king. Those days were rife with inter ethnic conflicts, and Dagbon and Yagbum (Gonjaland) constantly waged war against each other. Dariʒiɛʏu promised never to wage war against his mother's folk, but was conned into reneging on his promise by his paternal cousins who knew it was ominous for him to attack those he had promised not to wage war against, especially as they were his blood relations. When Dariʒiɛʏu realized what he had been tricked into doing, he said it would be cowardly to retreat from battle. He was killed in the ensuing fight. This is the scene captured by the verse quoted above, which is used to teach the moral of bravery in the face of imminent death. The drummers never left him even though they knew they would perish in that battle. They show unfailing loyalty; hence Dariʒiɛyu's progeny should reciprocate this constancy and show their gratitude by being generous to the drummers' grandchildren. This intertextuality connects discourses separated by centuries.

We need this background information in order to get to the root of this praise line. Barber (1999: 37) notes this when she says that special knowledge is required to understand African poetry, because 'meanings' are usually masked. Equipping oneself with the relevant public linguistic repertory is not necessarily an indication that one can avail oneself of this genre of poetry. Drummers allude to ancient history to get to the core of the story in the poem. Plus, one needs to be cognizant of what the natives consider good poetry. It is common to hear statements like "Drummer X knows how to sing, but his voice is not 'sweet', and drummer Y has a sweet voice but no expertise in 'singing'." That is to say, X has the song but not the voice, and Y the voice but not the song. A virtuosic performer is one who combines knowledge of both content and style of delivery, and as such can hold the attention of his audience through a night of epic poetry (*samban luŋa*). A melodic voice enhances the quality of the song, but that is not prerequisite to the praise song or music. Audiences will look for an amalgam of the two elements of repertory and style of delivery. Commenting on the place of affect, ornamentation, and voice quality DjeDje (2008: 18) echoes Shiloah's (1995: 16) that, the perfect musician is one who imprints his emotions on the listener's soul, and is "he who is moved and causes his listeners to be moved. Thus, in addition to his beautiful voice, tenderness and keen sensitivity often recur as basic qualities required from an excellent musician." Proverb lore is good for ornamentation, but these could be slanted. In the Ghanaweb of September 17 2008, under the title "Use of proverbs in news broadcasting condemned", the National Media Commission (NMC) meeting on language, in Kumasi, Ghana, observed that,

> "Participants . . . have condemned the use of proverbs in news items as they tend to breach journalistic tenets and could cause confusion in the run-up to the December general election. While affirming the importance of using local languages to reach the generality of Ghanaians not literate in the English Language, participants were, however, worried about the abusive use of proverbs thus rendering a slanted version of what is supposed to be a factual rendition of events. [The] ... use of proverbs [that] might provoke people to cause mayhem"

This underscores the potency of the spoken word, especially of veiled words that can be given multiple interpretations.

Ornamentation is central to poetry, and is a powerful tool of the poet. Poets will sometimes exaggerate in order to paint an awe inspiring heroic character. Issah Zɔhi, for example, says in his epic narration of Naa Luro's exploits that the hero's foe, Dajia broke nine bows, as opposed to Toombihi wulana's (another drummer) mentioning three bows; in a bid to show the type of stiff opposition their hero, Naa Luro, faced in battling the dimunitive but powerful Gonja warrior.

Praise poetry in Africa encompasses both panegyrics and epics. Belcher (1999: 16) notes that,

> Clan or lineage poems and songs of praise necessarily evoke clan history and the celebrated individuals of the past. The praise song may sometimes tell a story, as would an epic, although allusion and indirect reference are the typical tropes of panegyric. Further, praise songs are incorporated into epics in varying degrees, and they appear inextricable from certain aspects of the epic performance.

Samban luŋa, the epic poetry rendition session activates past time in the present, merging ancestors with their living relations, as a way of accessing accumulated powers. During the narration geography and history, that is, place and genealogy are intertwined. The narration begins from a venerable ancestor and recounts their achievements through to their passing, then linking them with the current chief. It is the practice to give ancestral place-origins as well as specific names of fathers and mothers[3]. Periods of reign of chiefs and kings serve as important points of reference for the people, and serve as the yardstick for drawing the timeline of events and Dagomba history. This is where the drummer is of primary importance as the historian and chronicler of present happenings. Like Sotho *lithoko*, Dagomba historical narrative views an idealized past time and laments the degeneration of heroic activity in today's world. It is common to hear a singer remind his patron that the good fortune he is enjoying has been bequeathed to him (and the general populace) by the ancestors, so he has to guide it jealously and not allow it to fall to pieces under his watch (see Salifu (2007: 112).) Some of the praise epithets have the same theme, e.g.,

> 1. Naa Luro:
> Ti dini ŋɔ (zabili) pa ni ti so shɛba dini.
> Our own this (battle) future will come-to better-than others own.
> Our's (battles/travails) will be better than others'.

Luro bemoans the degeneration of the times; yesterday was better than today, which will also be better than tomorrow.

> 2. Savilugu naa Bukali Kantanparim:
> Bɛ ti ku chɛ ma daŋ daa yibu, ka m baʋa shi kpalim gbe.
> They will not spare me precede market exit, and my care-less remain sleep-at-home.
> In these times of lawlessness no good ever comes out of any enterprise.

POESY AND RITUAL

Wherever praise singing is involved it suggests the existence of a praise singer and the praised, thereby evoking the existence of a hierarchy. When customary behavior makes statements about hierarchical relations between people we move into the realm of ritual; in this case, a ritual expression of

---

[3] In the extended family a father's siblings are all one's "fathers" just as one's mother's siblings are his/her "mothers." There is therefore no such word as "cousin" in Dagbani. Children of uncles and aunts are "brothers" and "sisters."

respect (see Richards (1956), Leach 1968, Goody, 1974: 39). In the field, I observed performances, but my analyses and interpretation will eventually be based on texts of these evanescent performances I observed, plus additional electronic and print media. These texts are double-sided instantiations, first of an intention to be interpreted, and then the presumption that the audience would anticipate this interpretation. We need to pay attention to culturally established modes of interpretation. Clues as to how texts should be interpreted are usually encoded in the body of the text. Where clues are not encoded, we need to have knowledge of antecedent texts which speak to issues raised within the present text, that is, look for intertextual relations with other texts.

We will need to place some praise epithets in their historical contexts to be able better appreciate them. In a virtual trading of proverbs, Naa Jɛngbariga's (reigned 1749-1772) son, Naa Ziblim Kulunku (ZK), reigned 1788-1806, chooses praise epithets to mock his cousin Savilugu naa Tampin Karili (TK), against whom he had competed for the *nam*. After his victory, the former says he is,

> 3. Kulunku laɣim kɔbiga ku ŋmani paaŋa.
> Kulunku gather hundred won't resemble cricket.
> A hundred little burrowing insects cannot match the cricket.

> 4. Silinchi kparigu mali viɛla, shɛriga m mali, ajojo kparigu mali viɛla, shɛriga m mali.
> Silk gown make beautiful, needle make, ajojo gown make beautiful, needle make.
> Every beautiful garment owes its beauty to the needle.

> 5. Ŋun bi su bini zabiri bini zuɣu, ka bindan bia wum n la n la n ti doni yɛliga.
> pansain. Yi Yɔɣu kpamba moomi yi nini bo bindan shee.
> Who not own thing fight thing because, and thing owner child hear laugh-laugh till lie on-back flat. You Dagbon elders redden your eyes find thing owner whereabouts.
> The usurper is obsessed with the prized property, and the rightful owner looks on in amusement. Elders of Dagbon, please seek the rightful owner.

> 6. Kinkaŋ buɣuli n yɛn nam, ka salinsaa pun pali naa puu ni tata.
> Wild fig grove about to create, and ant already numerous king inside absolutely.

Before the fig grove grows we already have ants residing therein.

Both Tampin Karili's father (Naa Ziblim Bandamda, reigned 1735-1749) and older brother, Naa Mahami Na'Kɔringa, 1772-1788, had taken consecutive turns at the Yani Kingship, so logically it was the Naa Andaan Jɛngbariga line that was entitled to the skin, yet Tampin Karili wanted to stampede his way through to the top. This, he fails to do, and when Naa Ziblim Kulunku eventually gets the coveted prize he decides to taunt Tampin Karili with these words, in order to drive home his message that no matter what T.K does he, ZK, would always out-perform him.

Tampin Karili in reply takes names as would console himself for the loss to Kulunku. He says,

7. Shɛba ni andun anu nu, shɛba ban yɛ ni andun pii pia, ashee Andun dahima

Dagbaŋnim ni ti yuri shɛli, ashee dina n zooi

Everyone names his price: Now I know that it is what Dagbon citizens want that they hold aloft.

To wit, T.K implies that no matter what one does, humans are wont to be inclined towards choices that will bring the most material gain to them. He feels he is the right choice, but the powers that be have decided to give the prize to a wealthier person.

KINESICS

Kinesic elements such as body posture during performance, voice modulation, and distance between singer and patron are important dynamics we will consider. The audience relies on these and other conventions that surround the generation of the text in order to both enjoy the music or praise, and grasp its meanings. Genre conventions thus intervene between performer/ creator and audience. Conventions are always continually revised between performer and audience. Young singers usually employ what Charry (2000: 94) calls the "beautiful" youthful voice, while the old musicians of the bardic tradition employ the "powerful" voice. This contrast in voice quality comes into sharp focus when the songs of Yakubu Salifu, a young *baamaaya* (a social dance) singer are juxtaposed with those of the older Timbobli and Timom. Yakubu, like his compatriots on the pop scene employs electrophones while the older performers only use the hour-glass and cylinderical bass drums.

Typically, young *lunsi* like Abdul-Rahman Baba and Banvim Lunnaa Ibrahim have this 'beautiful' youthful voice, while the older Adam Gbaɣu and Nyoligu Lunnaa Issahaku Mɔɣulo on the other have the 'powerful' voice.

In a cultural performance setting there could be as many as a hundred drummers, who will all follow a lead master drummer called the *lun'daa* 'male drum'. This drum calls and the rest of the drums in the ensemble respond. There is a second drum that cues the other drummers as they go along, and the master drummer continually improvises. There is so much cross- and poly-rhythms going on that many westerners misjudge the sound as cacophonous. The drums will "talk" among themselves as well as to patrons. They are said to talk because they mimic the tonal patterns of the Dagbani language. The interlocking beats of the drums, ululations, praise uttering, and rhythmic movements that accompany each performance generates social cohesion that is expressed in dance by the members of the audience. "This element of involvement, music, dance, and drama during the performance, the affective indices of the poet's voice and the paralinguistic aspects of his performance cannot be represented in the text," See Olatunji (1979: 181), and Small (1987: 50)[4]

The obscurity of praise poetry is a product of oral transmission and time passage which changes vocabulary, a loss of memory, semantic blurring and grammaticalization, among other things, contributing to this game of signification where meanings are created, secretted, and rewoven to suit particular contexts. This indicates that oral texts are objects of hermeneutic speculation where layered meanings are possible. This is the shaky ground upon which present day Dagombas walk when they are confronted with this esoteric literature of *salima*, which seems to stand at the crossroads between 'idealized' history, 'fantastic' folktales and present day reality. Some people dance to the rhythmic combination of song and drum without actually placing the words in proper context. The best scenario however happens when the target audience is able to place each performance in its proper context. This synergizes the efforts of performer and audience and renders the communication situation complete. Kumbun naa Issah Bla's praise line that draws on the folktale villainous character hyena will illustrate this.

    8. Kumbun naa Issah:

---

[4] He uses the term 'musicking' to describe this act of taking part in a musical performance, that is, an aggregate of the playing of musical instruments, singing, and dancing.

Sapili (Kunduŋ) piri kurugu namda m maan too kpiɛŋ.
Hyena wear metal shoes and again increase strength.
Hyena has worn a metallic shoe and added to his strength.

This needs to be placed in context, for the praise epithet was chosen at a specific period to describe the circumstance surrounding Issah's ascension to the Kumbuŋ skin. He refers to himself as the strong Hyena who has worn a metallic shoe and increased his strength. Here it is the Hyena's brute strength Issah has appropriated for his name, not its villainous trait of avarice. The history surrounding this name is that little-fancied Issah is given the chiefship of Kumbuŋ much to the chagrin of rival princes, who claimed he was a Gonja and unrelated to the Kumbuŋ skin. The colonial British administrator intervenes in the ensuing dispute and affirms that Issah is qualified, and confirms him chief of Kumbuŋ. It is this administrative endorsement that is referred to as the metallic shoe. Issah's foes can thus have no antidote to the double force of the iron-shoed hyena. Hyena (Issah) may not be liked by so-called humans (his foes), but when he combines his brute strength with the iron-shoes the colonial administrator clad him in, he becomes invincible. The word *sapili* is an old word for *kunduŋ* 'hyena', which is not found in present day vocabulary. It is the practice to refer to hyena in the salima genre by this older term.

9. Kumbun naa Yamusah (Zambaŋa) has the praise line,
Sapili kumdi ka zambaŋ taŋli.
Hyena crying and cat mute.
The cat (leopard) is not flustered by the howling of the hyena.

Taŋli is yet another archaic usage. The word in contemporary usage is *shini*. Yamusah calls himself the Leopard who cannot be harmed by the empty noises made by the cowardly hyena, that is, he has the bark and not the bite. A good performance does not only augur well for cultural continuity but also elevates the musician, because the story he has told is his.

The praise names inevitably revolve around the people's belief systems. Dagombas believe in the existence of witches, and every misfortune may be blamed on witches or evil spirits. Witches are usually women. In one such epithet, a chief of Karaga, Yinifa, couches a name that has this theme of witchcraft to speak of the fact that one should not cut off the hand that feeds him, in the proverbial name,

10. Pavasaribla mali pua ka gbaai pavadoviso tɔvinda ŋubi, ti yuuni ŋun yɛn deei bia o gbaa dali.

Maid has pregnancy and catch woman-birth-giving-attendant chew, we look-forward-to who will collect child her kneeling day.

A pregnant maid has killed the midwife; we await the day she will be in labor.

Dagbon praise poetry, like the Mexican corridos Paredes (1994)[5] talks of, alludes to historical facts, past or present, but unlike the corrido, Dagomba praise epithets and epic poetry is embellished. Voice quality and drumming skills act in tandem to determine a Dagomba drummer's stature. These songs are embellished by our drummers as part of their verbal artistry. A Dagomba drummer who does not embellish his poems is not seen as virtuosic. Abrahams (2000: 23) observes that folklore provides guidelines for behavior, in that,

> Expressive folklore assists in maintaining the status quo
> by giving a "name" to the threatening forces both within and
> without the group … in a contrived, artificial form and context,
> giving the impression that the forces are being controlled.

These praise epithets largely set out to maintain this status quo, of the royal versus the commoner. The commoner and the royal each have their place in society. A few examples of some chiefs[6] will help illustrate these:

11. Pivu lana Ziblim:

Kpaŋ bundana di lari suliga nandana, noo bundana di lari suliga nandana.

Guineafowl wealthy don't laugh-at hawk poor, hen wealthy don't laugh-at hawk poor

Tarim bundana, mira ka a diɛm nabi' nandana, o pa ni ti naagi a tabili a balibu.

Commoner wealthy desist from deriding prince poor, he future will finish you add-to your kind.

---

[5] See the Introduction to Americo Parèdes 1994. With His Pistol in His Hand. Austin: University of Texas Press.

[6] A chief is naa 'chief/king', or lana/dana 'owner'. Chief of town X will thus be X naa/ X lana, the chief of, or owner of the town.

Just as the poor hawk shall rule over the wealthy fowls, the poor prince who is mocked by the rich commoner will one day preside over all matters concerning the rich commoners who used to deride him.

The fortunes will reverse, for the poor royal will soon rule over the "powerless" rich commoner.

12. Naa Mahama Kpɛma:

Ŋun maviri di mori kamboŋ lana, kamboŋ lana ka mɔbu.

Who buys NEG IMP challenge silo owner, silo owner not-have challenging.

One who buys should not be rude to the food source. The owner of the silo is beyond challenge.

13. Pu'suvuli yi ŋmɛlim di ku ŋmani kamboŋ lana

Farm-hut if grow-fat it NEG resemble silo owner

No matter how large a farm hut is it cannot match the entrance hall of the King's house.

14. Savinari naa Sule:

Kaliwɔli ni paŋ mɔriti shɛm ŋɔ, di mɔriti ka dolila Naa Yaakubu zuu Yu'voli.

Nodule has borrowed swell how this, it swelling and follow Naa Yaakuba's ulcer hole.

(The nodule is a consequence of a wound, and should lay claim to the pain of the injury.)

The image cannot be the same as the original/ One should not cry louder than the bereaved.

15. Kambonnnaa Kojo Tabaraba:

Tarim je suli n tavim tavim vali.

Commoner get angry mumble mumble swallow.

The commoner seethes in anger, but cannot take any action (against the powerful).

These names seek to maintain the status quo. The commoner who does not know his rightful place will suffer the fate of an arrogant fowl in the court of the hawk. The king is ruler, and should be respected as such. This group of names also suggests that the society will be peaceful if everyone knew and accepted their stations in life. Much intra-ethnic strife in Dagbon, and indeed Ghana as a whole, is caused by non royals meddling in issues that are reserved for royals.

Also, there are praise names that address issues of virtue triumphing over vice. Truth is usually delineated as a tolerant persona who is plagued by falsehood. However, his resilience always pays off in the end and falsehood becomes the vanquished. Here are some examples of some chiefs' praise names,

16. Naa Mahama Bla:
Ʒiri laʋim kɔbiga, yɛlimaŋli ko n gari.
Lies sum-up hundred truth alone surpass.
One single truth is better than a hundred falsehoods.

17. Abdulai (Abudu) Naʋibiegu:
Yɛlmaŋa naaya ka guula yɛlimaŋ' dara, ŋun ti mali tu'saata ŋun' m mali yɛlmaŋli.
Truths are-finished and remain truths bought, who come-to have thousands three he has truth.
Real truth has ceased and bought truths have taken over. Only the rich are right now.

This does not however mean that he is advocating recourse to falsehood or bootlicking. The name is drawing our attention to the vanity of kowtowing to the whims and caprices of the affluent.

18. Naa Andaan Zoli Kuʋuli:
Ʒiri kɔri vuʋusi ka yɛlimaŋli bɔri bimbira shee.
Lies make ridges and truth seek seed location.
(Falsehood is yet ploughing his field (i.e., scheming), but truth has passed that stage and seeking to is plant his seeds.
Truth shall always triumph over falsehood.

19. Gushe' naa Iddi:
Ʒiri nyaʋisa pam, di labiga m biɛ.
Falsehood sweet a lot it return ugly.
Falsehood is sweet, but its end results are disastrous.
Think quality, not quantity.

20. Naa Yaakubu Andani:
Alibarika bini din pɔr' ni niŋ pam.
Blessed thing which small will become expansive.
The little thing that is blessed shall increase in size.

21. Kampakuya Naa Abdulai Yaakubu:
Suhuyini bini din' gbamda ku kpalim soli.
Patient thing that crawls won't remain road.
The patient one never gets lost enroute/ Patience is golden.

22. Shero zuu Gbuluŋ lana Iddi:
Ɖun gari ti nyeei kumdi mee mee, ka ŋun jɛndi zaa ŋɔ ŋun fa?
Who just touch crying mee mee what of who absolutely be part?
If the outsider takes up everything, what will the rightful owner say?

The wise is contrasted against the foolish in this next epithet,

23. Savilugu naa Bukali Kurivili:
Jɛrigu baa kariti wabiri ka o lara, ka wabigu baʏa be baa lana ni.
fool's dog chasing elephants and he laughs, but elephant care (not) be-in
dog owner in
The fool's dog is chasing elephants, (and he is hopeful of catching a big
game). The elephant is neither flustered by the dog nor its owner.

Vain pride and overreaching oneself is what this last epithet mocks.

Another popular theme one finds among the praise names is one that
shows a relationship between a beneficent leader and an appreciative follower.
These epithets make use of pairs of symbols where the lesser one gets its
sustenance from a bigger one, as can be found in these examples, where the
higher symbolic character is highlighted, and the lesser one underlined:

24. Vo' naa Kpaliga:
N duuma Naawuni chɛli kpaliga ka baŋli paai du
My lord God protect oak and lizard reach climb.
God protect the oak tree for the lizard will climb.

25. Gukpɛʏu Salaamba lana Issah:
Naawuni chɛli wulli, ka ti'zoo tabili paʏi Wuni
God leave branch and parasitic-plant stick praise God
It is a good tree branch that supports a parasitic plant

26. Naanton naa Sule Bla/ Gbuluŋ lana Mahama:
Dim' baa din tabili mɔʏuli, di ku yaʏisi palibu
Creek which beside river it not in-time fill-up
The creek that is close to the river will soon get full of water

27. Kɔrili lana Mahami Yaakubu (Nantoo's son)
Naawuni chɛli saha din' viɛla, ka so' chandiba chaŋ paɣi Wuni
God leave time which good and way-farers travel thank God
May God make the times good ones so that way farers will travel safely
and happily.

These epithets show their bearers' gratitude in being elevated to the
current positions, and their desire to be given higher titles in future. They show
deferential behavior to seniors, usually the superior chief or the Yaa Naa
himself, who made them grow in stature. In the oppositions we find in each
praise name we find the lower in status always receiving something out of the
mercy or magnanimity of the superior, that is,

Junior	Senior
lizard	oak
parasitic plant	tree branch
creek	river
wayfarers	good time

In espousing a theme of a strong force coming face to face with a weaker
one or a victor versus the vanquished, we see a profuse usage of predators and
animals they prey upon, or of lower animals making vain threats against
bigger ones. Examples include the following,

28. Issah Kunkuni (dana):
Zaanzana gbaai waliga, ka zaɣ maŋa gbahi gbuɣima. (See Dakpem
lunnaa.)
Cobwebs catch deer and type real catch lions.
If ordinary cobwebs can entrap deer then real ones will catch lions.
29. Bee yi kuli ŋmɛlim ka bo, di ku paai gbalipini.
Shin/leg if just grow-fat like what, it won't reach thigh.
No matter how large it grows, a leg cannot be as big as a thigh.
30. Gbuluŋ lana Yinifa:
Kunduŋ kuri kpani ni o ŋme gbuɣima.
Hyena fashion spear to strike lions.
The hyena has fashioned a spear to attack lions.

There are praise names that address the theme of death, either as an
equalizer, or an inevitable end for all humans. Diyali lana Dahamani has a

praise name that says rich or poor, we shall all dance the dance of death, and thus be equals.

31. Bundan' kuli ku mali wɔb'laa; di yi pa piɛ'laa, navila nav'laa.

Wealthy-person funeral won't perform bull-elephant; it if not ram then bull.

A wealthy person's funeral and an ordinary person's are observed in similar manner.

32. Tibuŋ lana Dawuni Kwaanawule:

Kum bi che binshavu.

Death not leave anything.

Death spares none.

33. Kojo Tabaraba:

Asaasi takoro obiaa ba ko [Twi].

Earth window everyone will go.

(All shall pass through the earth's window.= the grave)

No one can escape the grave. / All shall die, irrespective of stature.

Those that entreat the patron to persevere include,

34. Naa Zɔrikuli/ Gbiŋgbaliga lana Taayili:

Yuŋ sakpɛli sav' borili: A kpee yi ŋmaai ka di bara pam, a gba nyin kpaŋmi a maŋa n ŋmaai ka di gari o zuvu.

Night food morsel: your colleague if cut and it big very, you too IMP strive your self cut and it surpass his head.

Strive hard to outperform your competitor in what you do.

35. Kar' naa Adam:

A dindana je a, kpaŋmi a maŋa ka a dindana yu a.

Your enemy hate you, strive-hard your self that your enemy love you.

Your enemy hates you: if you work hard your enemy will love you

The philosophy of this poetic genre of *salima*, like the Homeric ethos[7] fathers' sent to their sons, is that their bearers are pre-eminent among others. These praise epithets are ethnopoetic and linguistic forms that not only express ideas, but also serve to influence society in many ways, socioliogical, economic, or political. Irvine (1989: 248) makes this same observation in her study of praise singing and the language and political economy in Wolof

---

[7] J. B. Hainsworth 1981: 25 quotes the line 'Always best and pre-eminent beyond all others' (Il., 6. 208;II. 784), as the words fathers would use to encourage bravery in battle.

society. She uses a Peircian semiotic approach whereby a linguistic phenomenon is used to serve many functions. She notes that,

> The consideration of language use and context has
> reached out to the material and historical conditions of linguistic
> performance. Thus, for example, linguists like William Labov portray
> speech as varying according to speakers' socioeconomic
> class and other affiliations relating to economic and political interest.
> The implication is that the class connotations of variants influence
> the direction of change in the linguistic system.

Both the chooser of the epithet and the poet who uses it seek to communicate a certain message, which will impact the community in a certain way. Linguistic objects and performances are exchanged for cash and goods, a situation in which there is a direct involvement of language in the political economy. It is this inter-relatedness of the world of objects, economic transactions, and political interests that interests us both.

PATERNAL AND MATERNAL LINEAGE

Both sides of a person's parental lineage are important in the praise singing genre. One cannot have a father but not a mother, and drummers will address both sides of our family trees. Dagbon society is a patrilineal one, where a child "belongs" to the father, yet his/her (the child's) draws his/her strength from the maternal relations. A child's maternal uncles will fortify him/her spiritually to avert any magical spells from enemies. Indeed there is no powerful personality whose maternal relations are not spiritually potent. The Dagomba society is polygynous. Many royal children share the same father whose position they all aspire to ascend to in the future, and would even try to undo each other in order to attain the title *X naa* (Chief X)[8]. Naa Zanjina (1648-1677) and Alhassan Tipariga (reigned 1899-1917) are addressed as,

> O zaŋla o bayili n diri nam ka zaŋ o mayili m puhiri jiŋli.
> He take his paternal lineage eat royalty and take his maternal lineage
> worship prayer.

---

[8] Siblings have been noted to resort to foul means to beat each other to the throne (skin). War and the use of sorcery have bedeviled this ancient institution of chieftaincy.

He has inherited his father's royalty, and his mother's humaneness.

This opaquely alludes to the two dimensions of the chief. He exhibits manly qualities of duty and service to the fatherland by virtue of being a true born son of his father, and shows a humane side which he has inherited from his god-fearing maternal lineage. This is similar to the male dominant patriarchal society Seitel (1980) observes among the Haya of Tanzania, where the hearth is the locus of the child's (and women's) world and the chief's palace is the centre of the political universe (the men's realm). In sex roles we have male principles of duty and obedience, and female principles of love and nurture.

CATEGORIES OF PRAISE SONGS

Praises come in different forms, and at different occasions. First, there are those praises that are uttered at chance, everyday meetings including markets, wedding and naming ceremonies. Single line, abbreviated praises are thrown at royals, for example, *kachaɣu bia* 'child of the female regent', *chɛ yuri bari kɔri yaaŋa* 'grandchild of (the one who) leaves horses and rides roan antelopes'. These are attention catching addressives that seek to draw the attention of the patron to the salutation of the bard, his ultimate aim being to attract some monetary reward.

Second, there are praises that are sung as part of a musical event. These are praise name songs that once belonged to ancestors and have now become part of the repertory of songs played for dancing. *Naani goo* 'trusted thorn', *naɣ'biɛɣu* 'awesome/ferocious bull', *kuli noli* 'the good watering hole' , *jɛŋkun' biɛɣu* 'ugly/wicked cat', *kɔndoliya, ti baŋ taba zuɣu dodo!* 'Now we know each other, caution is key.' In this second category of praises the singer begins by naming the ancestor who went by the name, and uses those words to address the dancer, who has requested to dance to that tune.

The third category, *biɛɣu naayo* "day break praise session", constitutes the Monday and Friday ritual praise sessions that symbolically wake the King up to pray. This is an Islamic practice that got incorporated into the tradition in the reign of Naa Zanjina, who brought Islam into Dagbon's politics. As a young man Zanjina travelled far and wide, and brought with him many innovations from Hausa land (which was largely Islamic). Similar practices are observed among the Manding (see Innes, 1976) and the Hausa (Smith, 1957).

Also of paramount importance are the praises that precede the performance of epic poetry *ʒiɛri tɔbu* 'sorting out the recipe' These are preludes to the main performance which serves to put the audience in the right frame of mind to take in the 'instruction' the teacher will give. An assistant to the master drummer leads this session, starting with *dakɔli n nyɛ bia ...* 'the bachelor is inferior to the married man'

As the narration proceeds, a fifth category of praises are introduced as asides during the narration, and directed to the patron. These are extraneous to the epic story, but tie present audiences to the personages in the epic story. Drummers use this conduit to address, criticize, or commend patrons. I heard a drummer address a patron thus at an epic poetry session in Yendi thus,

> Ka nyini ni tiri pini ka di niŋ anyaⱴisim shɛm ŋɔ, ka mani ŋun deeri ŋɔ ŋuni fa?
> If you the giver are this happy, what about I the recipient?

This is not overtly a praise epithet, but the subtle message is that the patron is benevolent, and is ever excited when he gives to others.

Another one tried to lure his audience to give more, by rebuking him in the following words:

> Miri ka a tiri pini ka samli ka a yɔra.
> Do not make presents as if you were paying a debt.

The logic in this latter saying is that people find it more difficult to part with money when repaying a debt, than they do when receiving it.

FEATURES OF PRAISE POETRY

Dagomba praise-poetry focuses not just on the potency of the person or entity it salutes, memorializes, or publicizes, but also pays attention to the narrative or linguistic continuity, to the effect that the singers will insist they have not added anything new to what their forebears 'fed' them with. They however agree that some songs are 'sweeter' because of the voice quality of the individual artist. The performance enhances the subject's political stature and aura, his/her social and political visibility.

The attributions bestowed onto the patron are rooted in names, appellations which could be sentential, and complex. Dakpɛm Nsuŋnaa's praise epithet,

Bɛ yɛ ni Tamali pala tiŋa; ti mi bi bɔli ba Tamali ka bɛ kana, ti yɛn ʒila kpe ka bɛ labi bɛ ya.

They say Tamale is no town: we did not invite them to Tamale, and we will still be here when they return to their homes,

is a complex sentence, and is critical of non-natives who say the city is a 'non-city', and is not worth living in, but yet find it hard to return to their own lands.

Table 4.1. Image Contrasts

Viewed positively	Perceived in Negative light
ours	Theirs
stay back	leave early
one cricket	a hundred burrowing insects
needle	beautiful garment
rightful owner	Usurper
ant(s)	a wild fig tree
poverty	Riches
strength	Weakness
cat (leopard)	Hyena
midwife	pregnant maid
poor hawk	wealthy guinea fowl
buyer	Seller
silo owner	farm hut
ulcer	Nodule
royal	Commoner
one truth	a hundred lies
real truths	bought truths
truthfulness/ seeds	falsehood/ridges
+sweetness	Bitterness
^little	Plentiful
+patient thing that crawls	will not remain enroute
rightful one	Acquaintance
elephant	the fool and his dog
+oak	Lizard
+branch	parasitic plant
andcreek	River
+good times	Wayfarers
real (snare) catching lions	cobwebs catching deer
thigh	Leg
lions	Hyena
+, = wealthy fellow's funeral; bull elephant	poor fellows funeral; Bull/ram
+, =death	all
+ earth's window	everyone
+ you	your colleague
you/ love	your enemy/ hate

+ Witty statement that does not contrast a clause that is seen in positive light against
  one that is perceived as negative or not so good.
^ Contrasts found, but both adjectives are co-referring to the same subject, and speak
  positively of it and symbiotic relationship between pair.
= equality of the pair.

Contrast is an important ingredient used in the representation of favored
and ridiculed persons targeted in the proverbial praise epithets. In this chapter,
we find contrasts between the following, as in Table 4.1.

PRAISE TYPES

When we look at the material drummers have used to refer to, address by,
narrate of, or sing about their patrons we come to identify the following types
of praises.

1. Single word praise terms. Single words such as *Gbuɣinli* 'lion', a
   praise term reserved for the King of Dagbon, *Wɔb' laa* 'Bull elephant'
   names the Chief of Gushaɣu, are used by drummers or court elders to
   catch the attention of their patron

2. Phrases. Like the single word epithets, phrasal appellations are used
   as attention grabbers. *Duniya balinda* 'earthly intercessor', *Bataŋ
   Zab'ʒirigu naa* 'Nantɔŋ warrior king', are both noun phrases and will
   be used to specifically refer to the Yaa Naa and the chief of Nantong
   respectively. *X dabuɣu' lana* 'inheritor of X', *Y zuu* 'Y's first born
   son', *chɛ ɣuri bari kɔri* 'leaves horses and rides roan antelopes'. The
   king of Dagbon, the Yaa Naa is also referred to as *kun/ŋun/ tiri ɣɛlli*
   'One who gives trouble'. My informant told me that the Overlord is
   compared to things that are unmatchable. No one compares to him
   and, before the modern state of Ghana came into being, it was he
   alone who can order that a person be sold into slavery, or executed.

3. Pet names/Nicknames. When they praise royalty, it is usual practice to
   occasionally use the pet names of patrons as addressives. Pet names
   used include *Gɔmma Shaara* for Yaakubu, *Zanjina Mankaana* for
   Mohammed/ Mahama', *Tooka and Dagara* = Abdulai', *daŋ tooni*
   'peerless one', Meemunatu is *Baamunu*, Alhassan is *Baako*, Ziblim is
   Munkaila, and Abukari is also affectionately called *Gariba*.

4. Sentential epithets. We also have those praise terms that are complete
   sentences, such as, *Man' daŋ biɛm (n tiligi saa mibu)* "I have

overcome malice", and *ka'bira bela zaŋ gu maŋa sivili* 'the little leftover grain is reserved for the lean season.' These are Andaan' Sivili's appellations. *Laringa yi kuli tam pia zuvu, jaambona awei ni sivisi o na* "if a squirrel rests on a high platform, nine clubs will bring it down."(Kumpati, the Gonja warrior)

5. Whole passages. The fifth category of praises involves those that span over several sentences, for example, in this epithet, Savnar' naa Sule's says his name is,

Ŋmaan ʒee nya kuvuloŋ ka turi baa ni o nangban suruŋ. Naawuni yi savira, kuvuloŋ ni doni tiŋa; ka ŋmaan ʒee niŋdi pɔndim pɔndim, ka o kari ti gbaagi o Gamanʒi dali.

When he has the slingshot the red monkey insults the dog's long mouth; we look forward to when the slingshot is put aside. It is then the monkey will be cringing, then the dog will pursue and catch him on that day of reckoning.

This paints a picture of a cowardly rival making ugly noise because he has some force backing him. When that support is withdrawn we shall see who the real man is. Whole length songs are also composed and addressed to individuals cataloging a chief's 'fathers' and 'mothers', that is, lineages of inter related siblings of their parents. When the praise names of these relations are uttered before patrons they are delighted to be associated with their forebears. Nyankal' lana Damba chooses the praise epithet,

M ba ka ya ŋɔ, m ma ka ya ŋɔ; ka bo lee tahi ma na? Kpalam bil gɔŋ n tahi ma na

My father absent town this, my mother absent town this; but what send me hither? Sack-small-curved bring me hither

Neither parent of mine is here; so how did I get here? My money got me here.

In the latter example, Damba is said to be descendent of a non Dagomba, but his hardwork gets him the Nyankpala skin. He taunts those who see him as a foreigner with this name, which eventually becomes a dance tune, like Naani goo and Navbievu.

6. Performance event as praise. Closely related to praise passages are occasions during which whole sessions such as an evening of epic poetry recitation 'samban luŋa', or a pre-dawn wake up drum session

'biɛɣu naayo', are used as a praise event. The practitioners say they want to use the occasion to pacify their patron.

The last category of praise has been at the core of recent clashes between rivals on the geo-political plane in Dagbon. There have been perennial incidences of fighting in the capital of the Dagbon state where the two rival gates lay claim to the throne. The epic rendition session is supposed to be held at the palace of the ruling king. This symbolizes his dominance in the kingdom. When there is a rival performance taking place in the same town his authority is questioned. No two lions can rein within the same pride. They will clash.

INTERTEXTUAL REFERENCES AND METACOMMUNICATION

Even more exciting to most patrons of royal praise singing is a category of praise where there is an oblique reference to another historical event during the presentation of a current narration. The current performance comes to reference a certain element whose existence may not be evident to those who lack the particular cultural history. Intertextuality, the relation of one text to another, pervades the genre of praise singing. A single text usually cannot be readily understood independently. In a dawn performance at the Kampakuya naa's forecourt, the drummer refers to Kampakuya naa (regent since 2006) as *Naɣbiɛɣu Siɣilana* 'inheritor/successor/incarnate to the fearsome cow'. This simple noun phrase carries a whole gamut of history, referring back to a period in the history of Dagbon when the land was ruled by Naa Abdulai Naɣbiɛɣu. Kampakuya naa not only goes by the birth name Abdulai, but also shares the same surname (Yaakubu), and grandfather's name (Andani) with Naɣbiɛɣu. Its metacommunicative dimension utilizes the unsaid messages the verbalized messages send to the patron. When he is told that, "Honey that has been placed in one's mouth is swallowed, not spat out," or called Naɣbiɛɣu's incarnate the real message is that he should not relinquish the throne to anyone, for like honey, the sweet throne is best kept for oneself as Naa Jiŋli and Naɣbiɛɣu[9] did before him.

---

[9] Both moved from regency to monarchy passing their uncles over.

The reflexivity between the text (verbal, drummed or written) and its world, make them dependant on each other for contextuality and interpretation. Each performance is a situated discourse, with a unique character, though it may bear resemblances to other performances by the same actor (or by others) at a different place and time. Quoting Foley (1986: 6-9), Tarkka (170) again asserts that, "text is the product of interpretation, more a process of meaning than an object." Intertextuality is a sequel to textuality. Oral modes of communication, more than written ones, make intertextuality easy to catch in their use of redundancy, formulaic expressions, metaphor, and nonverbal signs and cues in intertextual networks of association and connotation. Tarkka then goes on to note that, it is "variation" that makes the relations between texts intertextual. Variation is a network within which performances find themselves. Notions of an original, historical, or ideal to be varied upon, come up when we think of 'variation'. "The analysis can be extended to such intertextual fields that only help the present reading of the text but were probably unknown to the singer or the interpretive community", Tarkka (ibid: 175) Babcock (1984).

Conventions and Interpretation of Praise Names

Salima are vocative in address and name-like in form. The lexical items in a name may be internally disjunctive, or be in relation to others. These condensed appellations are allusive in reference. *Chɛ yuri bari kɔri* 'leave horses and ride roan antelopes' for example, is a praise line for the Sunson naa. It is a condensed form of a historical event in which a past chief of Sunsɔŋ, felt he was too strong to ride a 'tame' horse. The more nimble footed antelope is the mount that befits him; but this mount ran amok and trampled him to his death in the wild. Praise epithets could be stanzaic, like southern African praise-poetry, or not, and single line *salima* can be expanded into *samban luŋa* 'narrative history' at a later event. One needs to have the historical and cultural knowledge, kin emblems as well as the details of the content of the hinterland to fully decipher the praise name.

Drummers as the performers of praise songs and epic poetry, as we have seen in the foregoing discussion, engage in a discourse that links the present to the past, viewing the two as a continuum. The wisdom of the old and whatever they have bequeathed to the present generation whose responsibility it is to keep the culture alive should not be laid to waste. If patrons actually relish being addressed by the praise epithets of their forebears it behooves them to rise up to the veiled challenge encoded in the message being delivered to them, in the same way the Yoruba *oriki* Irvine (1989: 39) talks of speak to patrons:

> Oriki encapsulates, in a name, your essential being, your most
> Cherished identity: but they also describe the parameters of the
> space into which you must expand – 'living up to' or reaching
> out into the horizons the name assigns.

Praise names in Dagbon are relished not just for their cognitive value, but for their affective function. They are the ingredients that elevate the epic above a mere chronicling of events, so that the repetition of the praise names as the narration progresses stirs the blood and makes the listener swell with pride.

In the wake up performance, biɛɣu naayo, (see Appendix 1), we see an explication of these two functions. The performance event as a whole is a metaphor of the relationship between the king/leader and his subordinates. The venue has to be in the fore court of the King's palace. Ordinary citizens, however affluent they are, are not permitted to organize a similar event at their homes. The citizenry thus converge at the king's house to watch the performance. This is a rallying ground where the culture is performed and enjoyed.

Biɛɣu naayo is a wakeup call to the ruler to rise up to the onerous task placed in his hands. The chant observed in this case, was directed at the regent of Dagbaŋ, Kampakuya naa Abdulai Yaakubu Andani, and his sister, the female regent Paɣaba lana Sanaatu Yaakubu Andani, in the wake of the burial of their deceased father, naa Yaakubu Andani. The story recounted by the drummer is that of the immediate past Yaa naa. I recall with a sense of nostalgia the day I interviewed one of the elders of the Yaa naa Yaakubu Andani in 1998, when I was on a research trip to Yendi. I enquired to know if he had any special praise song like those I heard of Dagbaŋ's heroes. I was told his 'story' would not be 'sweet' since he was still alive. I never imagined the time for me to hear his song would come four years thence, when the king was assassinated, and I would have the opportunity of hearing drummers chant his story.

In this song, the drummer recounts the tortuous journey Naa Andani Zɔli, Yaakubu's father, took to get to the final destination of Yani. This I saw as a well researched enterprise, for I am conversant with the story, as outlined in the Ollenu Commission's report[10]. The committee reversed a previous court's decision, and asked that the then King Naa Mahamadu Abdulai (1968-1974) be removed from office, and paved way for the enskinment of Naa Andani's regent Yakubu (reigned 1974-2002) as the new King.

In his opening line, Luŋ Issah Zɔhi beseeches the new regent, Kampakuya naa Abdulai Yaakubu with the words,

> Miri ka a ti ʒini ka Kulikpuni kom zo n chɛ ŋama.
> Be-cautious that you be seated and Kulikpuni water run leave hippos.
> Exercise caution, lest the waters of the Kulikpuni River will recede and leave hippos stranded.

This statement is a two pronged sword. It tells the new overlord he is powerful, but he should exercise some restraint in his deeds, for they have far reaching consequences. He should not also get complacent that he has the ultimate prize and sleep on the job. He cannot afford to be caught napping, for the drummer tells him, *sokam kpalimi a nuu ni* "all and sundry are now under your dominion and protection". He appeals to tradition to corroborate his story. What he is saying is not a figment of his imagination, so he tells his audience that the regent's endorsement transcends the traditional Dagomba boundaries. The traditional authorities as represented by the two most senior traditional authorities of Dagbaŋ in the absence of a substantive king - the Kuvu naa and the Zɔhi naa-, affirm what he says, just as much as the United Nations and the Government of Ghana (the President and his Vice President) do. They have imbued the Kampakuya naa with the authority that the Regent of Dagbaŋ commands. He is told that if all these powerful fellows say he is regent he has no one to fear but God Almighty. This apart, the patron is given some advice to the effect that as a leader he should be accommodating, and desist from listening to idle gossip.

The drummers' importance as the educator, entertainer, historian and collective archivist of the society cannot be overemphasized. This is the reason their art will ever live. The flip side has them inflaming passions when they use their poetic license to say otherwise "unsayable" things, or asking patrons to act rashly.

---

[10] This was the committee appointed to investigate the anomalies in the ascension to the Yani skin, on April 23, 1974 by the government of the National Redemption Council of Gen. I. K. Acheampong.

Chapter 5

WHAT IS IN THE PRAISE NAME, POSITIVE OR NEGATIVE LORE?

> From time immemorial, men have relished the delights of verbal warfare. It is a paradox of our own inarticulate age that this enjoyment of a clever insult has never been higher. Having largely lost our interest in using language with precision and imagination, we hide our real thoughts behind fuzzy words and a mealy mouth – but we secretly admire those who have the courage to say aloud what we ourselves only dare to think[1]
>
> Nancy McPhee

Dagombas assert that drummers have the "facts" about historical and social realities and have through their art preserved over five hundred years of folk history (Chernoff 1997: 96). When drummers acknowledge a patron by "saluting" him/her with praises, or go to wake the king up on Monday and Friday[2] mornings, they engage in a ritual of greetings; rituals during which past and present personages are collapsed into one and the same. The eulogies both salute and recognize present (the living) and erstwhile (departed) noble presences. At burial ceremonies of chiefs, drumming the praises of the departed will make the deceased rest in peace. It is believed the soul of the departed will not leave this upper world if it is not given the required drum-dirge accompanied by its praises. S/he is then told *donimi balim ka tiŋ maai*

---

[1] See foreword to Nancy McPhee 1978: 7.
[2] This is an Islamic influence. The two days are sacred ones, hence he is reminded he needs God'd protection for a prosperous economy.

'lie perfectly still (rest in peace) for calm to prevail'. Firth (1974: 16) recognizes the social significance of this encounter by saying that

> Greeting rituals imply a positive acceptance of the person met, a willingness to establish a social relationship; [and] parting rituals imply a recognition that the relationship has been established, and some hint that it could continue.

At social functions such as durbars, funerals and festivals drummers play a third party function, by publicizing whoever is present. They 'introduce' each person to others in much the same way as a third-party mutually known to two strangers needs to introduce them to each other in Western society.

Figure 5.1. Drummer saluting Chief (in white) as he arrives at a durbar.

Body posture and position or proximity are very important in their interaction too. When a chief sits in state, his drummer draws close to him and kneels in front of him, if he will not be masked by others in the crowd. In a large crowd, a drummer with his jaw resting in his palm and head tilted to one side, draws close and stares his patron in the eye. The drummer then makes sure he keeps his patron engaged by not losing eye contact, and salutes him with his praise epithets. This is when the patron is told *lu yumi tiba wum a bayili yɛlli* 'open your ears and listen to matters pertaining to your paternity.' This is a direct imperative which borders on a command. No one other than his beloved 'wives' uses such imperatives when they speak to the king, as it will be discourteous, and face threatening. When saluting a noble person, a drummer draws close to him/her and maintains eye contact, but will kneel or sit on the ground when addressing a deceased one (see figures 5.1 and 5.2 respectively). These are symptomatic of the general Dagomba signals of respect for the elderly, or of higher ranking persons than one. Whereas 5.1 has a cheerful air 5.2 has a solemn ambience around it.

Figure 5.2. Drummers show humility by sitting, to mourn a deceased chief.

PRAISE NAMES

In the names following, personalities come to be associated with praise epithets they choose for themselves or inherit from their forebears, much in the same way as nicknames get associated with people. From my observation, I see these names to be rhythmic, poetic, humorous, witty, or derogatory.

The words of the praise name invariably draw on a comparison of a sort between humans, animals, or artifacts, with a view to presenting the target of praise as the better of the pair if s/he is presented in positive light or the worse (or not so good) one if s/he is to be lampooned or asked to rise up to their responsibilities. At a first glance, we are tempted to conclude that whatever goes into the making of a praise name or song, the intent is to prompt to a certain kind of action; asking the patron and by extension their descendants to emulate heroic behavior and shun cowardice, be morally upright, or pour scorn on their enemies. This 'name calling' tradition among Dagomba royals functions like the Mexican corridos. While encouraging heroic behavior they caution against irrational behavior. According to McDowell (2000: 16) there is,

> ample evidence that young men in the ballad communities
> emulate heroic behavior as presented in the songs . . . [and there is] an
> urge to reflect on the legitimate and illegitimate uses of violence, to assess the
> consequences of violent actions,
> and to assign a broader meaning to violent episodes that have
> disturbed the social equilibrium.

These are the two dimensions - a call to emulate the positive, and a warning to shun the negative - we will be looking at in our present discussion of *salima*. A major principle at play in the choice of praise names is the regard for social space. One must not violate the norm by choosing a name that will disrespect a higher chief, one from whom s/he will in the future approach for a higher position. The choice of a name that affronts one's senior is akin to shooting one's self in the foot. One needs to pay close attention to the avoidance as well as the presentational rituals (see Goffman 1956), as a means to deferring to seniors. What are the actions when put up will amount to invasions of social space? These need to be avoided in order to maintain peace and calm.

In chapter four we saw that praise names, which are proverbial or allusive in nature, challenge patrons to live above reproach, strive hard to achieve higher laurels, or they taunt and lampoon rivals or perceived enemies. A name thus makes a statement of relationship between the person who "owns" or associates with it, and others. The praise poem is a ritual statement that embodies the soul of the person(s) it salutes, ritually saluting their bearers and those related to them. (Also see Leach (1954), Arhin (1986: 164).

When drummers salute a patrons with their praise names when they meet, their action functions the same way as an opening greeting seeks to open a sequence of communicative acts between persons, same as Esther Goody (1974: 40) observes among the Gonja. These initial salutatory appellations function as the opening to social intercourses, so that the delivery of any messages or information can then take place. The drummer again uses parting praises to give the occasion a coda.

THE POLITICAL SIGNIFICANCE OF THE PRAISE POEMS

A person is given a *suuna/dɔyiri yuli* 'birth name', what John McDowell (1981) calls a "legal name" when s/he is born. The birth name is used throughout life, unless the bearer takes a chietaincy title or epithet later on in life. Grow up, especially toward adolescence, they may acquire a pet or derogatory name, "*yu' paa*", depending on their countenance or personalities, and when they become chiefs they are then required to choose another name, a praise epithet that will come to be associated with their chieftaincy titles. When they acquire these titles, it is impolite to address them by their first names. In Dagomba life, the nickname usually fades away when the person reaches adulthood, and is almost not used when he becomes a chief. McDowell (1981: 2) talks of a similar personal system of naming among the Kamsá where there are four personal reference and address forms (a legal name, a kinship term, a garden name, and an ugly name). The Dagomba praise epithet is not quite the same as the Kamsá garden name, but is affectionately called one's *da' kabiri soli yuli* "the name s/he is known by, by peers when on the way to the bush to gather faggots", or a *kuliga soli yuli* "the riverside name", that is to say the name my peers know me by. This name is usually one that distinguishes one as a witty person, a reason why one has to be cautious when choosing a name that presents him/her as one mightier than his/her seniors.

Dagbon praise poetry identifies the King (Yaa Naa) with the entire Dagbon nation. The Yaa Naa is an amiable personality who balances his power with love for his people. He is father of the Nation, the ideal king. As the embodiment of the whole nation, the king is all powerful; he can raise the lowly and humble the mighty. He is the awesome *Gbuyunli* "Lion", but as the *duniya balinda* "Earth's intercessor/One the whole populace intercedes with" he is the one who intercedes with the gods on behalf of the general populace, while at the same time everyone is at his mercy. His ruthlessness is balanced by his protective nature over his dominion. He is father to all, that is,

Ban mali laamba ba/biɛli, bɛn ka laamba ba/biɛli.
Those have owners father/older sibling, those lack owners father/older sibling.
Protector of those with homes and those without homes (the homeless ie. natives and strangers).

Being the overlord it is his duty to see to it that all under his domain are well protected and catered for. Again, he clothes the nation,

> Gunsi ni sɔmbu bela naa Gbewaa nuu ni.
> Silk cotton trees and ginneries be king Gbewaa hand in.
> King Gbewaa controls the fabric with which the land is clothed (He clothes the populace).

Arhin (1986: 169) uses similar adjectives to describe the Asante king. The poems present him as a hero, a fearsome and fearless fighter of great strength and nimble movements. He is a ruthless strategist capable of great mental and physical endurance, unpredictable, dependable, and pitiless. The Yaa Naa is also *ŋun tiri yiɛlli* "the one who causes harms.", that is, he can order any sort of punishment be meted out to anyone.

Samban luŋa as a term encompasses the epic, eulogies and salutations to patrons. The term also is used to name the entire performance event, during which the drummer collapses time, drawing a remote historical past close to the present. In his story, he makes the historical personage synonymous with the present occupier of the political position, much in the same way as Scheub (2002: xi) notes that in the story, ". . . time collapses and we are in the presence of history . . ." The chief literally sits on the same skin his mythic ancestor once sat on, and is kept in physical contact by associating with (sitting on) the royal skin. We find these in the following excerpt from an epic session performed by the drummer Luŋ Issah Zɔhi, at the palace of the regent of Dagbon:

> Spirit of Oratory, speak so that I may learn to speak.
> [ululations and praise terms addressed to griot(s)]
> Father, speak so that I may learn to speak . . .
> Oratory is my birth right, I don't doubt it (I am no imposter).
> The one who possesses should enjoy, Sovereign one,
> The one who lacks should relax, Sovereign one, . . .
> Whoever claims Almighty God is not King,
> That fellow should look in front and behind, . . .
> That fellow should examine a single cloth and tell its front from the back . . .
> That fellow should take a bee's wax and tell the front from the back, . . .
> And know that God really is King, Fraternity!
> It is you, who created Man,
> And then created man's hands to join the arms

And created the earth's trees,…
It is you, who created the mighty mountain,
The unclimbable mountain that is best circumnavigated.
It is you, who created the expansive river,
The river closes the door to stop the termite.
The young pupil holds his Qur'an (script) to study,
He studies and calls to God, the omnipotent.
When the (sorghum) farmer picks up his hoe,
He farms and cries to God, the Almighty.
When the warrior (hunter) picks up his weapon
And enters the bush, he looks up to God, Almighty,
When the ginner picks up her bow to card cotton
She gins and looks up to God the almighty,
The carver too, when he holds a pestle in his hands,
He cries to God, Almighty.

You are the one who kills the wealthy and take away their treasures
You are the one who kills the poor and take their poverty from them,
You are the one, who eventually makes the owner of a small house the owner of a mansion,
And turn the owner of a mansion into the owner of a small house.
You are the one who turns a bachelor into a husband of ten wives
And make a husband of ten wives a bachelor.
Which king can match King God? He is the Almighty!
It is you, who created the horse rider,
But when fellow riders are mounted he runs on the ground
It is you who created the owner of food[3]
But when his colleagues feast, he goes to lick their dishes (pick crumbs).
It is you, who created the meat eater,
Yet when fellow canivores are feasting he only has bones to break,
He chews and looks up to God, there is none like Him.
It is you, who makes a slave a royal in another land,
And make a royal a slave in another country.
Which king can match King God? Thus does the Almighty work!

Spirit of Oratory! Softly, Softly!
My beloved, first son born of an alien woman!
I am going to carry hearth stones to cook the ceremonial meal.
This first born son of the alien woman is a trail blazer,

---

[3] *Sa Yim lana* 'owner of food/ the sustainer' is an appellation for the King of Dagbon.

Your mercies, your mercies!
King Nyɛriga, tread and there be calm on Earth!
King Nyɛriga, sit and let there be calm, Earth's carrier!
Man is not God,
Man is not God, so say I the son of a drummer!
I will proceed to remember my father's grandfather.
Spirit of Oratory!
My forebear wisely hung around King Zavili
And his first son Nyavsi proceeded to be king from regency.

The day King Nyavisi ascended the throne,
Floods settled into ponds,
And went on to become a spring, and sand turned into a mountain,
I am the one who stirs the dry corn meal
King Nyavisi brought in his royal wives,

Spirit of my father!
Play and let others dance,
The one who drums to educate mankind is a royal
My father, the drum is grateful, is his name.
Is there a soul that will not age?
Ageing is a natural phenomenon
King Nyavisi fought stealthily,
And got to Gaa that day,
And when Gaa folk heard of him, they all fled,
Leaving behind a headstrong boy, to watch over the monkey-guava tree,
And when the king descended beneath the tree that day,
And the child ate and threw some dry fruits on the king,
And the king raised his head and looked and saw the child,
And ordered that they bring the child down,
And they brought the child down,
And he asked the child, where are your townsfolk?

And he said that: "My Lord, we always come to eat these fruits,
But today I came and did not see anyone."
And the king got a white robe and robed the child that day,
And got a hooded cape and adorned the child that day,
And got a staff and gave to the child that day,
And took him and made him Gaa chief,
And we say Gaa Tuviɛligu chief's father is Shitɔbu's son King Nyavisi
Zinyee chief Asachi's father,
Nyavisi's female regent Kachavu

Dipala chief Nyaŋzi's father, King Nyavisi, son of Shitɔbu

Nyavisi's female regent Kachavu,

Tibuŋ chief Timalli's father, King Nyavisi

Siŋa chief Lali yɔvu's father, King Nyavisi

Daluŋ chief, one cannot force one's will on another person's child's father, King Nyavisi,

Savilugu chief, the one who sits high on the throne, KingNyavisi's son,

Kumbunnaa is the awesome one, King Nyavisi's son,

Tɔlin chief, God's Mercies, father is KingNyavisi,

Savnarigu chief, who is that has no enemy, father is Naa Nyavisi,

Zuvu chief, who is king of dancing's father, KingNyavisi,

Banvim chief the Alpha, King Nyavisi son,

Gukpiɛvu chief Tulebi's father, King Nyavisi,

Saŋ chief, the hoe-handle's father,

Zabzuvu chief Salt's father, King Nyavisi,

Nanton chief's father, King Nyavisi

The head drummer, Bizuŋ's father, King Nyavisi

My ancestor Bizuŋ was a prince of Dagbon

But turned himself into one who entreats

Entreats at dusk and entreats till daybreak; beseaching the king will not go unrewarded.

He precedes the king to the royal shed

Amid the morning thunder-claps of his lead drum

And the supporting drums drone like mosquitoes

And all say that is the Prince Bizuŋ

Bizuŋ describes how the king burns grass and how he fishes…

And when the king rides his horse Malimali Bizuŋ rides Malimali's tail (is right behind)

Then when the king rides Fast-horse-with-a-mane

My grandfather follows right behind The Maned One

And then when the king rides Red-horse-does-not-farm,

My grandfather is right behind, …

And grandfather Bizuŋ strived and begot his royal sons.

N.B: it is standard practice in the praise singing, or narration to immediately follow up with patrons' or a town's praise epithets after their names have been mentioned. I have underlined these epithets in the excerpt above.

The drummer in this prelude to the narration, not only enumerates past kings and their children, but seeks to link these personages to the regent. There is no distinction between the sacred and the mundane; both worlds merge, with God almighty controlling the earth through the rulers. We also see him trace the drummers' link to royalty. The historian is no commoner, he too ascribes to some royalty. His pleas, he asserts will always be rewarded. The strength of the chief is the commoner just as much as the the strength of the commoner is the chief, a symbiotic relationship that is highlighted by the drummers when they use their craft to show the historical continuity of the ethnic group by linking the commoner to a royal ancestor.

The drummer selects images that seem unrelated and then establishes bonds between them. These externalized images draw the audience, emotionally, making it possible for the 'creation' of myth, "Myth[4] is in the images, music in the connections: the result is metaphor." These metaphors are so powerful and captivating that many a Dagomba royal will sacrifice anything to be the one at the focus of a performance, whether directly or by association, through an ancestor. In their description of the lives of culture heroes drummers present a "heroic literature [that] conforms to set patterns of behavior reflective of the society's worldview" (See Johnson, 1992: 2). In the world of Dagombas there is a drummer caste, and a ruler class. Issah alludes to this distribution of labor when he says,

> Spirit of my father,
> Play and let others dance.

He also enumerates some of the age-old professions in Dagbon (pupil (representative of the Islamic scholar/ education), farming, hunting, textile industry, pottery, and carving). He will enumerate more professions depending on the time at his disposal. Drummers are the descendants of his father, and the "others" referred to here are the royals.

In this chant the drummer poet utilizes parrellel constructions juxtaposed with repetitions of fixed phrases, for example,

> Spirit of Oratory, speak so that I may learn to speak.
> Father, speak so that I may learn to speak . . .

---

[4] The Encarta dictionary defines *Myth* as "a traditional story about heroes or supernatural beings, often attempting to explain the origins of natural phenomena or aspects of human behavior."

Spirit of oratory and *father* occupy the same X-slot in the paradigm in the phrase "X, speak so that I may learn to speak." The recurrent sentence structure is of the form "whoever claims almighty God is not king, then that fellow should do Y: where Y is an act that is beyond human capability." When human artisans set out to perform any task, they look up to God also.

> Whoever claims Almighty God is not king
> That fellow should look in front and behind.

There are always oppositions between "bachelor" and "the married", "man/creation" and "God/creator", "superior/the strong" and "inferior/the weak", "front" and "behind".

We also find in the excerpts links between images and their human correlates, and the imagery of power as represented by the symbols of Dagomba authority (in bold characters), below:

> And the king got a white robe and robed the child that day,
> And got a hooded cape and adorned the child that day,
> And got a staff and gave to the child that day,
> And took him and made him Gaa chief,

The hooded cape, staff and robe are all royal regalia. Following from ancestraltradition, the singer imbues his song with equestrian images of riders (rulers) and those who tarry along on foot (commoners). The Almighty's majesty manifests in his wondrous creations, which are used metonymically to refer to Him. These images are those of God, the "mighty, unclimbable mountain", and "expansive river", who is impervious to the machinations of the vain "termite", that is, man.

After addressing the Almighty, the awe-inspiring King is next in the hierarchy. In paying tribute to him the drummer says there was chaos before Nyaɣisi became king, but calm was restored as soon as he ascended the throne. Other nations fled when they heard him coming.

> The day King Nyaʋisi ascended the throne,
> Floods settled into ponds,
> And went on to become a spring, and sand turned into a mountain,

The drummer, who is both storyteller and praise singer, thus artistically draws the audience into the heart of the story, couching their memories of experience in metaphor, myth, and music, making the audience participants, not mere listeners, or observers. He utilizes rhetorical questions as well as direct addressives to God, ancestors, and his patron to give the narration a tone of immediacy.

MYTH AND TRANSFORMATION

The epic stories the drummers narrate are so suffused with myths and legends that one is transmuted to a fantastic world of sorts when one finds oneself at a performance setting. The two terms, *myth* and *legend* need some definition here. In the literature, a legend is said to be a historical narrative that combines fact and fiction, and differs from a myth by portraying a human hero rather than one who is a god. Myth is generally seen as 'sacred history' of primordal time. Scheub (2002: 185) quotes Eliade (1968: 6-7) as saying that,

> . . . myth tells how, through the deeds of Supernatural Beings, a
> reality comes into existence . . . Myth, then, is always an account
> of a 'creation'; it relates how something was produced, began to be.
> Myth is a story that has to do with first causes, origins, a story of
> cosmological transformations.

Myth and legend come to be one in this realm of the Dagomba cosmology, for the historical personages become sacred entities, and deities. I disagree with Blair (see Duncan-Johnstone 1930: 12) when he says that "the Drum History of Dagomba bears the marks of legend, rather than myth." He suggests that the tales told are exaggerated, or false. I do agree that there is some embellishment, yet the narrations are true and, in fact, are sometimes corroborated by narrations from neighboring cultures. As the drummer narrates his mytho-legendary tale, which is re-created in each performance, he presents a saga of the struggle between antithetical forces, those of order and chaos. His hero is representative of order, and all that is good, while the hero's foe is the most villanous of characters. Myth, as the realm of the unknowable, is poetically linked to human experience. The drummer-cum-storyteller often employs ambiguity and irony in a dynamic manner to give his audience this transmutation of corpus that has been remolded to fit contemporary needs in their retellings. His narratives are often mysterious and metaphorical, calling for a "willing suspension of disbelief" in order to move along with the story.

The regenerative power of memory that is kindled by praise poetry evokes the sense of belonging and patriotism. Like the *izimbongi* of South Africa (see

Gunner 1999: 52-3), *lunsi* collapse this heroic past into the heroic present through song their songs.

PRAISE NAMES

Many of the praise names draw on a chooser's ability to coin a proverbial line or text that passes on some wit or advice. Luŋ Salifu sings the praise epithet of the chief of Tibuŋ lana Adama, which says,

> Suhu ni kpamli n gari paliginli/ŋun paligi
> Heart in age better-than greyness/ who grey
> What is in the heart is better than the external features

While noting the premium placed on the wisdom of the aged, this epithet tells its audience that mere grey hair does not make a wise person. Wisdom is a thing of the heart, and we thus have to look into people's substance and respect them for what they are worth.

One of Tolin naa Suleman Bila's epithets is,

> Dun nyɛ biɛla baŋ malibu, di ni niŋ pam
> Who get little know keeping it will become plenty
> If managed well, one can multiply what was little.

This obviously advises its audience to manage their resources well. They should not be wasteful.

NAMES THAT 'FRICK': PRAISES DESCRIBED AS POSITIVE NAMES

Nicknames are used to either 'frick' or 'prick'. *Frick* is a Ghanaian slang word that means 'pleasurable'. Whatever praise epithet one takes for oneself one seeks to derive some pleasure from this choice; some choices are however double-edged swords that please their choosers and simultaneously hurt or incense others. Positive names are those names that espouse positive themes and neither malign nor offend others. These are the names that will help build a nation, those that will build a nation of healthy relations.

In the following praise name of Naa Zɔkuli told to me by my primary informant, for example, we find such positive use of praise names.

> Yuŋ saʋkpɛrili: a kpee yi ŋmaai ka di bara, a gba nyin kpaŋimi a maŋa n ŋmaai
> Night food-morsel your colleague if cut and it big you too you(IMP) strive your self cut
> ka di gari o dini.
> and it surpass his own.
> (A morsel of food: if a competitor cuts a large morsel, ensure that you cut a larger one than his/hers.)
> Settle for nothing other than the best.

The exhortation is that we should strive to surpass what our competitors achieve and not be envious. In a praise song, the warrior-bard Mohammed Adenchi sings his patron's praise name,

> Kpaliŋmaŋ sua, gbiriga gbiriga pa ni taai.
> Dawadawa-chest knife wobbly wobbly eventually will light-up.
> A blunt knife that is constantly used will get sharp.

The moral here is that, perseverance will bring success. Tamale Dakpɛma Nasaɣiri (Mbiniwaya)'s epithet,

> Tadabo tia ku puhi nyaʋili.
> Ink-tree won't put-forth-buds (ink) pods.
> The black berry tree does not bear ink fruits.

gives very useful advice to the effect that, this tree produces the sap that is used to make ink, but one has to make an effort in order to get the finished product. Nothing good ever comes on a silver platter. Such positive names which frick their audiences and also give good advice are, to say the least, what the society needs.

Positive names will not be the main focus here, not because they do not 'prick' their bearers to do things they should be doing. A lot of scholarship has already gone into the use of (positive) praise poetry, so we will concentrate more on the negative aspects. We need to throw more light on the negative, so that we can seek ways of reforming the system of praising.

PRAISES THAT ARE OF A SEXUAL NATURE OR USE PROFANE LANGUAGE

Praise names that encode sexual images are very characteristic of the warrior clan, drummers, and persons who are deemed to be brazen and do not shy away from sexually suggestive language. These are people who have the ceremonial license to use language in forms that are not permissible to others. Goffman (1956: 494) notes that,

> some playful profanation seems to be directed not so
> much at outsiders as at the recipient himself, by way of
> lightly teasing him or testing ritual limits in regard to him.
> It should be said that in our society this kind of play is directed
> by adults to those of lesser ceremonial breed – to children,
> old people, servants, and so forth . . .

If the message presented by the profane praise epithet is perceived in positive light by people who are higher up on the social ladder the bearer will escape sanctions that might be associated with such profanation in the presence of 'elders'. The opposite occurs if the sexual image is meant to incense a particular target in the community. These are the potentially explosive devices in the society, whose explosion will prick others. We find this latter dimension in Nyaanshe' naa Tim Biɛyu's praise name,

> Bɔ' guli kɔŋ sua, ka laribakonim nyɛri bindi.
> Farm watcher lack knife and yams ease feces.
> (The farm hand lacks a knife and yam tubers defecate in his face)
> An impotent man poses no threat to the women in a harem.

where he intimates that his foes are eunuchs, the worst possible insult one can hurl at a man. In Dagomba practice persons who keep watch over farm produce can eat part thereof when they are hungry. Yellow yam (symbolizes the female genitalia in this proverb) is a special species of yam, but the watchman lacks a knife (penis/potency), that is, the tool to peel or cut it.

PRAISE EPITHETS WITH SEXUAL IMAGES

These epithets are those that present sexual images or use sexually implicit language. They have been compiled from the body of praise epithets found in the general corpus I have collected in the course of my study, from various drummers and recorded performances.

Tampiuŋ Lunnaa Yidaantɔɣima/ Tɔŋ Lun' naa Tisua, son of Namo' naa Ashaɣu:

1. Kɔɣu napɔŋ tɔɣisi pani ku chibi voli.
Roan antelope leg imitate vulva won't pierce hole.
Though the antelope's foot is shaped like the vulva it does not have what it takes to be a vagina.
MORAL: An imitation cannot be like the original)

Mogulo
2. Jɔɣu ni bini: Yo' zuɣu yi kuli mali viɛli waayo di yɛn kpela pani ni.
Groin in thing: penis head if just clean beautiful how it will enter vagina in
A thing of the groin: no matter how cleansed the prepuce is, it is meant for the vagina.
MORAL: Everything has its purpose in life.

Manguli lana Kofi:
3. N ni zaŋ binshaɣu kam ti sana, amaa zaŋ m paɣa ti sana ŋuna, yɛla kam niŋda, din' ku niŋ!
I will take everything give guest, but take my wife give guest, things all possible, that won't happen!
Courtesies extended to a guest do not include sleeping with my wife
MORAL: I will not give more than I should.

Gbolo naa Tikuli:
4. Gbalipina sɔŋ gbina, ka gbina niŋ pɔrilo.
Thighs help buttocks and buttocks do curvy.
Heavy thighs make the poterior curvier.
MORAL: COMPLIMENTARITY; Teamwork will always win.

Tampiuŋ Lunnaa Yidaantɔɣima:
5. Pan' kɔbiri sɔŋ pani ka pani niŋ nura.
Vulva hairs assist vulva and vulva become chubby.
Pubic hair has helped make the vulva chubby.

MORAL: Teamwork wins.

6. *Ziŋguya ku kpiɛli taba.*
Clitorises won't wedge each other.
It takes a man a woman to make love.
MORAL: Teamwork wins.

Nyaanshe' naa Tim Biɛɣu:
7. *Bɔ' guli kɔŋ sua, ka laribakonim nyɛri bindi.*
Farm watcher lack knife and yams ease feces.
The farm hand lacks a knife and yam tubers defecate in his face.
 = the impotent man is 'harmless' to a harem of beautiful women.
MORAL: One cannot perform a task one is not well equipped to do.

Naa Dimani:
8. *Bɛ sa gɔli ma yuŋ ku yina mɔli.*
They yesterday make-love-to me night NOT come-out broadcast.
One does not publicize one's sex life.
MORAL: Do not make everything public. Some things are better kept
secret.

9. *Pan' nyɛbiri duu ku pihi chɛrili.*
Vulva intercourse room will not find crumb.
We do not pick up crumbs in a room where we have sexual intercourse.
MORAL: Verile/ I am capable

10. *Pani kpabili nyɛbi ku sa.*
Vulva shut make-love will not run-diarrhea.
A tight vagina does not induce diarrhea.
MORAL: I am capable of performing arduous tasks.

11. *Pani Maliɛɣu ku firigi nuu, naɣila yɔli.*
Vulva mushroom NOT unstuck hand except penis.
It is with a penis, not a hand, which we uproot the mushroom that resides
in the vagina.
MORAL: Use a specific tool for the specific job.

Naa Yɛnzoo:
12. *Pa'gɔrili ŋma n gbaai zaŋ tiri gooni.*
Maiden block and catch take put across wall.
One sneaks into the house with a lecherous woman he has secretly
courted.

MORAL: Live virtuous lives/An illegitimate thing cannot be openly displayed.

Andaan Jɛngbariga:

13. *Nantariga kpuɣi bantibo pakɔli, bɛ yaa pa ni ti mali taba: bin' nyɔma balibu.*

Mole take smelly-insect widow, they as-usual will hold each other : things smelly kind

Mole has married the smelly insect's widow; leave them alone with their smells.

14. *Girigintɔli dɔɣi bia n zaŋ-puhi nɔŋ ni o yoli, bɛ yaa pa ni ti mali taba: bin' tɔri balibu.*

Scorpion specie born child give-to scorpion to foster, they as usual will have each other: venomous folk.

One species of scorpion gives birth to a child and given it to another to foster. Leave them alone with their venom.

MORAL: They are one of a kind.

Kar' naa Yinifa:

15. *Paɣasaribla mali pua ka gbaai paɣadoɣiso-tɔɣinda ŋubi. Ti yuuni ŋun yɛn deei bia o gbaa dali.*

Maid has pregnancy and catch midwife chew. We looking who will collect child her kneeling day.

The pregnant maid has killed the midwife; we look forward to the day she will get into labor.

MORAL: We shall see the results on the day of reckoning.

Chɔɣu naa Nayi:

16. *Paɣisaribila sɔɣiri yoli ku sɔɣi pua.*

Maid hide penis won't hide pregnancy.

The maid who secretly has sex cannot hide the ensuing pregnancy.

MORAL: Whatever is done in secret will come to light eventually

Gushe' naa Adirikarili:

17. *Pa'gɔrili dini m mɔri, ka nachimba ŋmaai daa ni.*

Maid knee swell and young-men cut market in.

The maid has a swollen knee and her suitors have ceased coming to the market.

MORAL: People driven by their selfish interests.

Gushe naa Gaani:

18. *Bin' biɛɣu ni saɣimjɔɣu. Na pɔli n kpejɔɣu ni.*
Thing ugly will destroy groin (royal hernia enter groin in).
The royal hernia has destroyed the groin and there is no remedy.
MORAL: Efforts to curb an incurable ailment will be in vain.

Banvim lana Mahami Kookali:
19.*Pumpɔŋɔ pan' bila bi ʒɛmda.*
Now vagina small not underestimated.
In contemporary times we do not underestimate a young vagina.
MORAL: These are strange, unusual times.

Chɔɣu naa Andani:
20. *Paɣ' biɛɣu daɣiri, zaŋ kpalim sɔɣiso ni.*
Woman ugly dirt take remain sponge in.
No amount of cleaning can cleanse an ugly (evil) person
MORAL: Shun the evil person/ not easy to detect.

Zangbalin naa Dayiŋa:
21. *Paɣ' biɛɣu dundoli zaŋ chibi gooni.*
Woman ugly gate take penetrate wall
The ugly wife is usually discriminated against.
MORAL: Do not discriminate.

Nabiyɔŋ lana Meeŋa, Chɔɣu naa Bineeti's son:
22. *Paɣ'biɛɣu mamli, salangbarigu, nye' nyɔnigu!*
Woman-ugly love, awful, incensing.
Do not court an ugly woman in secret: she will want to be acknowledged, much to her suitor's annoyance.
MORAL: Do not do what you do not want others to know of.

Galwei lana Aduna:
23. *Paɣa zaɣisi o maam, o ku yɛli o shira.*
Woman refuse her lover, she will not tell her friend.
A woman seldom informs others when her love breaks up.
MORAL: Everyone has a right to their privacy/secrets.

Nabiyɔŋ Achiika:
24. *Dagɔr' jɛrigu nyuri bara o maam tooni. Bɛ ni gbaagi a ka a maam la, n-lahi kɔhi, n ti a maam ka o di.*
Man foolish drink empty-challenge his lover front. They will arrest you and your lover laugh, again sell you, and give your lover and she eat.

The foolish male exhibits vanity in a woman's presence. She will profit from your woes.

MORAL: Beware of vain pride, and the treachery of loved ones.

Dimal' lana Musah = Sagnar' naa Bukali Kpɛma's son:

25. Dakɔli yoli ku luɣusi vɔli ni.

Bachelor penis won't scoop out hole in.

A bachelor shall also find love.

MORAL: Never despair, be hopeful..

Chaankpɛm lana Busaviri:

26. Paɣasaribihi wuhirila gbuna, ka nachimba be kambon waa ni.

Ladies show-off buttocks and young men be-in war dance.

While the young ladies are exhibiting beauty the brave men are ready for battle.

MORAL: Bravery/ courage [while others waste time on trivial issues 'men' address serious issues].

Kumbun' naa Suleman' Kpɛma:

27. Paɣ'dɔɣiso gbuni kun saai tɔm.

New mother bottom won't lack bitterness.

A woman newly delivered of a baby hardly forgets what pain is.

MORAL : Who feels it knows it most.

Naluŋ Yɛrinaa:

28. Fɔn' pa'gɔrili ni saɣim puli.

Urban woman roamer will spoil stomach

A city-dweller maid aborts her pregnancy.

MORAL: City life is not always the best.

Sabal' Yɛrinaa Yamusah:

29. Nanim' n chɛ paɣaba yɛla, tarimba miri ka bɛ mali karimbaani

Kings leave women matter commoners desist that they have pride

Kings are powerless against women not to talk of commoners.

MORAL: Never underestimate the power of a woman

Zɔɣu lana Suleman Kpɛma:

30. Paɣa gbaai doo nuu ni kun dam kpeeni.

Woman hold man hand cannot stir hard.

When a woman holds a man's hand he becomes powerless.

MORAL: Woman is powerful/ No man is beyond the power of a womaan's charm.

Banvim lana Nayindoo:
31. Gbin'chu'yalim ku gari bia.
Buttock-gourd-width won't surpass child
The big posterior cannot be more important than a baby. (Beauty is meaningless without progeny)
MORAL: Children are a blessing.

Among the thirty-two praises that use sexually explicit or implicit language, 9 mention vagina/vulva, 3 penis, 1 clitoris, 2 bachelor, 14 (lecherous) woman, 4 buttocks, and making love 5. The strong person is the virile, sexually active person, usually a man, so that when he associates with sexual symbols or language that makes him stand tall among peers, he blows his ego to superhuman standards. The sensual flavor given to these epithets does not take away from the authority they carry. In spite of their apparent profanity they present an array of themes, both friendly and antagonistic

These range from those that address "imitation" [1], "doing/ using the right thing/tool" [2, 3, 11], "complementarity" [4, 5, 6], "taunts" [7, 13, 14, 15, 16, 27], "be circumspect in whatever you do" [8, 17, 24], "capable person" [9, 10], "live virtuous lives/ issues of morality" [12, 18, 20, 22, 23, 25, 29], "woman is powerful" [30, 31], and "beauty is useless without progeny" [32].

In sum, the sexual idiom the praise epithets use equates a sexually potent character, or one who associates with such themes through their reference to sex, to a strong character and personality, the imitator is the less-than-potent person, and the 'macho, sensual man' is the original.

NAMES THAT PRICK: "NEGATIVE NAMES"

A negative name is a salutation that either explicitly or obliquely hurts the feelings of another. These names may lampoon, cast insinuations at others, or depict them as lower in stature than the bearer of the name. Oftentimes, these names do not name names but speak in generic terms. They are targeted at specific persons in the community, who are able to discern the hidden insult, challenge or proverbial language that is intended for them, and this serves as ingredient for conflict. This conflict leads to a 'battle', which can assume many forms — battle of words, physical warfare, or recourse to sorcery. Metaphor and idiomatic language are the principal poetic devices used in salima. Metaphor is an implicit comparison of persons or things, that is, one thing used or considered to represent another. The common metaphor used in this genre is that of strength, where a strong animal triumphs over a weaker one. The Yaa Naa is the Lion, the king of the forest. A foe, for example, may be described as vermin, or a cowardly creature.

PRAISE NAMES THAT CAST INSINUATIONS

The epithets in this category subtly address an opponent in non-complimentary terms. They speak in general terms, but are really targeted at foes that the proverbial epithet couches as envious, wicked, vain, nonentities, foolish or covetous. Examples include the following personalities:

Naa Birigu Yɔmda:
32. Zamba piliya ka di shee waɣa.
Wickedness start and its place long.
Wickedness has long been here with us.

Naa Andan Sivili:
33. Ba, she ŋun nye o (karimbaan) bindi ni va o karimbaan bindi.
Dog type who defecate his impudence feces will pick up his impudent feces.
The dog who impudently defecates at a prohibited place will clean up its feces.

Bukali Tampiŋ Karili:
34. Dagbaŋnim ni yuri shɛli, ashee di kɔŋko n kuli zooi? Shɛba yɛlimi ni andun anunu,
Dagombas if love something, i-see it alone just mighty? Some say that five five,
shɛba ni andun piipia, a ti shee andun dahima.
some that ten-ten, little-knowing wealth.
Whoever has wealth has everything.

35. Sa'kurili yi bu a di so ni saa maligim (bu a).
Rain-big if beat you it better-than that rain dew (beat you).
It is better to be drenched by rain than to be made wet by dew.

Yɛlizoli lana Dasan' Kpɛma:
36. Salinsaa nyɛ liɣiri n zaɣisi ni o da kakpiri ka doli dari kpana, amii bo ka o yɛn ŋme Naɣlɔɣu yili?

Ant get money refuse for him buy seed sorghum and follow buy spears,
I-wonder what that he will hit Naɣlɔɣu house.

The ant has gotten rich and is amassing arms instead of buying sorghum;
I wonder who he is going to fight at Yɛlizoli.

Yɛlizoli lana Yidaantɔɣima:
37. Pakura ŋubiri waayo ku ŋubi gballi.
Old-women chew virtuoso NOT chew grave.
A dreaded witch has no power over a grave.

Naantonnaa Yinifa (Bahiga):
38. Gumachuɣu turi gingalli ni o nagban' ŋmaliŋ, ka nyin zuɣu tabiliŋ la?
Chameleon insult snail that his mouth crooked, what-of your head oblong DET.
The oblong-headed chameleon should not abuse the crooked mouth of the snail.

Saɣnar' naa Sule:
39. Ŋmaan ʒee nya kuɣulɔŋ ka turi baa ni o nangban suruŋ; Naawuni yi saɣira, kuɣulɔŋ ni doni tiŋa; ka ŋmaan ʒee niŋdi pɔndim pɔndim, ka o kari ti gbaagi o Gamanʒi dali.
When he has the slingshot the red monkey insults the dog's long mouth; we look forward to when the slingshot is put aside. It is then the monkey will be cringing, then the dog will pursue and catch him on that day of reckoning.

Saɣnar' naa Ziblim:
40. Gampiriga pihi vari ka di biɛri shia, shia ŋun taachi.
Fir shoot leaves and it pain 'shia' tree, shia his nature.
The shia tree characteristically envies the shade of the fir tree.

Vɔɣu lana Mahama:
41. Jɛrigu n yɛli ni o ko, ashee ti zaa dunia.
Fool says that he alone, not-knowing we all world.
The fool deludes himself that he owns the world, little knowing it is for us all.

Vo' naa Bukali:
42. N kpee nya ma tiri zuŋ, tiri zuŋ ku gbaai ma.
My peer see me point zuŋ, point zuŋ will-not catch me.
My enemy has seen me and is unhappy but cannot harm me.

Zuɣu lana Simaani:
43. Nabihi je ma ka m mi be bɛ sunsuuni cha!
Royals hate me and I too be their midst aha!
My peers detest me but I stand tall in their midst.

Saŋ lana Yaakubu:
44. Tintani zaɣisi zɔmia, ka zɔmia gɔri o gama.
Bare-land refuse creeping-plant but creeping-plant roams its strength.
The ground has refused to support the creeping plant, but he grows on
his own.

Banvim lana Mahama Kookali:
45. Jɛrigu chaŋ daa n zaɣisi o daŋnim kalibu ka dɔli kaanila
bundaamba, daa yi yi o ni kuli o kɔŋko; bin' munli.
Fool go market refuse his family counting and follow counting wealthy,
market if exit he will return his alone; oaf.
One who hero-worships shall always be a loser.

Diyali lana Mahama:
46. Bɛ chimla bɛ vi, bɛ ni ŋubi bɛ vi.
They fry their shame, they will chew their shame.
They have done a shameful deed and will bear the consequences.

Gbuluŋ lana Alhassan Bla:
47. Gutuli ku sooŋa n ŋmaligi tam wɔb' kuri yɛla.
Ingrate kill rabbit turn forget elephant killer matter.
The braggart who has only killed a rabbit has forgotten that another has
killed an elephant.

Gbuluŋ lana Naantogma:
48. Bɛ borimi ni n yɛli, m bi yɛli, bɛ ku baŋ ma.
They want that I talk, I not talk, they won't know me.
They want me to talk; I haven't talked, they cannot know my position.

This is an insinuation he is using to carry his frustration to an intended
audience. Why did he not just shut up if he did not want to say anything?

Tolin naa Doozo:
49. Ba' jɛrigu gbaai sulli, di ka dabaayi ni ata ka o bɔri ni o gbaai yo'naa
mini o bia.

Dog-fool catch hawk, it not-be 2 days and 3 and he want that he catch bush-king and his child.
The foolish dog who has caught a hawk is deluding himself he can catch a lion.

Tɔlin naa Abla Bla:
50. Ti baŋ taba zuvu dodo.
We know each-other head upright.
Now we know each other, we shall all be cautious.

Woribɔvu lana Yinifa:
51. ʒin nya nya o buni, di biɛri Yɔvunim ku gbaai fa.
Never had has his wealth, it pain Dagbon-folk cannot collect seize.
No one can seize my newfound wealth.

Zangbaliŋ lana Aduna:
52. Zamba kɔbiga niŋdi Aduna bo? Di niŋdi Guŋ pava bia banzabanza.
Wickedness hundred do Aduna what? It do Guŋ woman child nothing.
No amount of wickedness can harm Aduna.

Dakpɛm Nsuŋnaa:
53. Bɛ yɛ ni Tamali pala tiŋa; ti mi bi bɔli ba Tamali ka bɛ kana, ti yɛn ʒila kpe ka bɛ labi bɛ ya.
They say Tamale is no town: we did not invite them to Tamale, and we will still be here when they return to their homes.

Chɔvu naa Bineeti:
54. A je ma nyabu ka n kanna, nyin pɔbimi a nini ka n garima, nin ŋuba lana bia.
You hate me seeing and I coming, you shut your eye and I passing, eye slit owner child.
If you do not want to see me, shut your eyes when I pass, you slit-eyed fellow.

Chɔvu naa Nayi:
55. Nyina lana (kunduŋ) che kɔbili yɛla, laanban sala lana (yiŋ baa) di mali karimbaani
Teeth owner (hyena) leave bone matter, gum slippery owner (domestic dog) shouldn't have impudence.
The dog should not pretend he can break a bone the hyena has abandoned.

In these epithets we see a constant use of symbols that contrast a good patron with an opponent who is variously described as wicked, a shitty and impudent dog, toothless, a witch, covetous fool, hero worshipper, envious fellow, ingrate, among others.

PRAISE NAMES THAT ARE INSULTS/LAMPOONS/INSINUATIONS OR DEROGATORY

Insults, both open and subtle, form part of the negative lore I call negative names. Where there is a comparison in a praise name, the target is always addressed as the inferior, and is usually seen as cowardly, foolish, slavish, impudent, covetous, or an ugly usurper. These epithets typify insulting praise name:

> Naa Niŋmitooni:
> 1. Ba' lɔvu zuli wali sinsaba, ka ŋmaan' dɔvu bɔri dibu ka zɔri baa bɔbili.
> Dog-male tail bear edible-berries, and monkey-male want eating but fear dog bullying.
> The bulldog's tail has born fruits; the monkey wants to eat but is afraid of the dog's sanctions.

The bull dog (speaker) is a courageous, strong personality who has the cherished prize which the coward (rival) wants, but dares not touch.

> Naa (Tim)tituviri:
> 2. Zabav' bilaa bia kami mɔvili ka yuee kani (Blaa bia kari mɔvili ka saa ku ni o mi).
> Gonja slave child drain river and nothing be-in (Slave child drains river and rain clouds to it rain.
> The Gonja slave strives in vain, for he cannot empty the waters of the river.

> Ŋmampirigu naa Dawura:
> 3. Bɛ che nini n ti jɛrigu ka jɛrigu turi niriba.
> They leave face give fool and fool abuse people.
> The fool abuses others because he has not been sanctioned.

> Naa Zanjina:
> 4. Suligbaŋ nya wɔb laa zoli m balisi balisi gbe mɔvuni.

Hawk see elephant male afterbirth stalk-stalk sleep bush.
A flock of hawks have struggled in vain to eat an elephant's afterbirth.
[To wit, if he becomes King rival ethnic groups will not be able to match his Kingdom.]

5. *Na' bin biɛvu maani kuli, o ku zaŋ buvuli.*
King mean performs funeral, he won't take shrine.
A greedy king inherits the property of the deceased, but not the responsibility that goes with it.

In this epithet zanjina casts the insinuation that a flock of hawks (his brothers and cousins) travail in vain for a prize, an elephant, but what they are actually struggling for is the afterbirth, which they cannot eat. He Zanjina already has the baby elephant in his possession.

Kumpati ku ŋubi sabili:
6. *Laringa yi tabi pia zuvu, jaambɔna awei ni sivisi o na.*
Squirrel if perch platform on, clubs nine will bring-down him here.
A club will bring down the squirrel perching on a height.
7. *Tandɔvu lɔŋ kum bɔli saa, saa mi ni bu o.*
Quarry-trench frog cry call rain, rain too will thrash him.
The frog in the creek has dared rain; rain will thrash him.

Naantɔn naa Suhu bɛri bo "What-ails-the-heart?" (Do' kuvu):
8. *Nachimba nɔli yɛli yiŋ ku yɛli mɔvuni.*
Young men mouth speak home won't speak bush.
People make ugly noises when they know there are others around to protect them.

Naa Andan Sivili:
9. *Ba, she ŋun nye o (karimbaan) bindi ni va o karimbaan bindi.*
Dog type who defecate his impudence feces will pick up his impudent feces.
The dog who impudently defecates at a prohibited place will clean up its feces.

Naa Ziblim Kulinku:
10. *Ɖun bi su bini zabiri bini zuvu, ka bindan bia wum n la n la n ti doni yɛliga pansain.*
Who not own thing fight thing because, and owner hear laugh-laugh lie face up Ideo.

The intruder is obsessed with another person's property, but the rightful owner looks on in amusement knowing that the usurper will lose out eventually.

Naa Alhassan (Katini) Tipariga:

11. *Ʒim taai kuliga/kurugu, ka chichɛnsi wɔlim je.*
Blood consume river/metal, and vermin struggle tire.
The river/iron rod is all bloodied and the vermin struggle in vain (they cannot eat it).

Naa Abudu(lai) Satankuvili:

12. *Jɛrigu yɛ ni di ni niŋ; di yɛn niŋ ka nyin kpe ya?*
Fool say that it will happen; it will happen and yoy enter where?
The fool says it should happen. Where will you hide when it happens?

Naa Andani Zɔli Kuvili:

13. *Tɔli bini ka sakɔvu kpuvi/zaŋ.*
Locust thing that grasshopper take.
The grasshopper has taken what belongs to the locust.

Saviligu lana Dahamani Kulikarijee:

14. *Jɛrigu kala yɛm maani dɔvim ka leei mali yɛm ŋmari dɔvim.*
Fool lack wisdom repair family but indeed have wisdom break family.
The fool has no wisdom to repair, but has one which will destroy his family.

Miɛŋ lana Alhassan:

15. *Ŋun bɔri Allaasani ka Allaasani bɔra, ŋun je Allaasani nangban pɔŋ.*
Who love Allaasani that Alaasani love, who hate Allaasani mouth rotten.
Allaasani loves those who love him; whoever hates him has a foul breath.

Yɛlizoli lana Asimaan Chuvu:

16. *Kɔŋ' n nya o data n vuri kpub kpub, ka vuri tɔbu, amii o leei yɛn tɔmi bee o yɛn labi mi?*
Leper see his rival and crawl and drag bow, I-wonder he will shoot or he will throw?
A leper has seen his rival and begins to drag a bow. Is he is going to hurl the bow at him, or can he shoot a bow and arrow?

17. Zin-nyɛri nya shaʋu zuʋu n doli turi mɔʋa, ka Yɔʋu kpamba suhuri Naawuni tiri sa'wuu zanibu dali, ka biɛŋ kom ti nyuui ka che mɔʋa kom; ka zin-nyɛri yɛn ʒini tarigi ʒinibu, ka kuli vuri pali pali ka vuri yuli, ka ʒi' suŋ leei goo n ŋmaligi kuhi o.

A cripple sees the flooded creek and insults the distant river. We await the dry season, to see where he will drink from.

Yɛlizoli lana Dasan' Kpɛma:

18. Salinsaa nyɛ liʋiri n zaʋisi ni o da kakpiri ka doli dari kpana, amii bo ka o yɛn ŋme Naʋlɔʋu yili?

Ant get money refuse for him buy seed sorghum and follow buy spears, I-wonder what that he will hit Naʋlɔʋu house.

The ant has gotten rich and is amassing arms instead of buying sorghum; I wonder who he is going to fight at Yɛlizoli.

Yɛlizoli lana Yidaantɔʋima:

19. Pakura ŋubiri waayo ku ŋubi gballi.

Old-women chew virtuoso NOT chew grave.

A dreaded witch has no power over a grave.

Naantonnaa Yinifa (Bahiga):

20. Gumachuʋu turi gingalli ni o nagban' ŋmaliŋ, ka nyin zuʋu tabiliŋ la?

Chameleon insult snail that his mouth crooked, what-of your head oblong DET.

The oblong-headed chameleon should not abuse the crooked mouth of the snail.

Saʋnar' naa Sule:

21. Ɖmaan ʒee nya kuʋulɔŋ ka turi baa ni o nangban suruŋ; Naawuni yi saʋira, kuʋulɔŋ ni doni tiŋa; ka ŋmaan ʒee niŋdi pɔndim pɔndim, ka o kari ti gbaagi o Gamanʒi dali

When he has the slingshot the red monkey insults the dog's long mouth; we look forward to when the slingshot is put aside. It is then the monkey will be cringing, then the dog will pursue and catch him on that day of reckoning.

Saʋnar' naa Ziblim:

22. Gampiriga pihi vari ka di biɛri shia, shia ŋun taachi.

Fir shoot leaves and it pain 'shia' tree, shia his nature.

The shia tree characteristically envies the shade of the fir tree.

Vɔɣu lana Mahama:

23. Jɛrigu n yɛli ni o ko, ashee ti zaa dunia.

Fool says that he alone, not-knowing we all world.

The fool deludes himself that he owns the world, little knowing it is for
us all.

Zuɣu lana Simaani:

24. Nabihi je ma ka m mi be bɛ sunsuuni cha!

Royals hate me and I too be their midst aha!

My peers detest me but I stand tall in their midst.

Saŋ lana Yaakubu:

25. Tintani zaɣisi zɔmia, ka zɔmia gɔri o gama.

Bare-land refuse creeping-plant but creeping-plant roams its strength.

The ground has refused to support the creeping plant, but he grows on
his own.

Banvim lana Mahama Kookali:

26. Jɛrigu chaŋ daa n zaɣisi o daŋnim kalibu ka dɔli kaanila
bundaamba, daa yi yi o ni kuli o kɔŋko; bin' munli

Fool go market refuse his family counting and follow counting wealthy,
market if exit he will return his alone; oaf.

One who hero-worships shall always be a loser.

27. N yi kuli bi so so amaa n so Kpataribo naa nim bana.

I if just not better-than anyone but I better-than Kpataribo naa folk them.

At least I am better than the chief of Kpataribɔɣu.

Epithet 27 is cast in the same mode as Guyanese in group speech play
tantalisin[5], see Edwards (1979). It was meant to be taken as a joke between
cousins, for Kpataribo naa's mother was Kookali's father's sister. There is a
cross-cousin joking relationship at play in Dagbon, where brothers' and
sisters' children have the license to poke fun at each other.

Diyali lana Mahama:

29. Bɛ chimla bɛ vi, bɛ ni ŋubi bɛ vi.

They fry their shame, they will chew their shame.

They have done a shameful deed and will bear the consequences.

---

[5] This is a Guyanese game of wit, linguistic artistry among ingroup members, where they trade
insults.

29. Tikub' bɔrila yɛla wumbu, ka lahi kana n ti bɔri yɛla chɔmbu.

Hypocrite love matters hearing, but again come to want matters sabotaging.

The hypocrite loves to listen to, but at the same time loves to sabotage matters.

Kumbun naa Zakali:

30. Kandinim dabari zaana Kɔro.

Kandi-folk deserted-compounds institutor, Kɔro.

Koro, the annihilator of Kandi folk.

31. Zakali daa ŋmanila zunzuuli bindi kɔbiri Kpɛvu dali, ka ŋmani buɤ'nooŋa kum bɔli tindaamba, ka ŋmani wanzam n pindi o taba (bihi) zuɤuri.

Zakali was like a hairy caterpillar during the Kpɛvu battle, and like a sacred bird that calls the priests, and like a barber who shaves his peers (i.e. beheads them).

Gbuluŋ lana Alhassan Bla:

32. Gutuli ku sooŋa n ŋmaligi tam wɔb' kuri yɛla.

Ingrate kill rabbit turn forget elephant killer matter.

The braggart who has only killed a rabbit has forgotten that another has killed an elephant.

Gbuluŋ lana Naantogma:

33. Bɛ borimi ni n yɛli, m bi yɛli, bɛ ku baŋ ma.

They want that I talk, I not talk, they won't know me.

They want me to talk; I haven't talked, they cannot know my position.

Tolin naa Doozo:

34. Ba' jɛrigu gbaai sulli, di ka dabaayi ni ata ka o bɔri ni o gbaai yo'naa mini o bia

Dog-fool catch hawk, it not-be 2 days and 3 and he want that he catch bush-king and his child.

The foolish dog who has caught a hawk is deluding himself he can catch a lion.

Tɔlin naa Abla Bla:

35. Ti baŋ taba zuɤu dodo.

We know each-other head upright.

Now we know each other, we shall all be cautious.

Wɔribɔɣu lana Yinifa:

36. ʒin nya nya o buni, di biɛri Yɔɣunim ku gbaai fa.

Never had has his wealth, it pain Dagbon-folk cannot collect seize.

No one can seize my newfound wealth.

PRAISE NAMES THAT DESCRIBE PATRONS AS MIGHTIER THAN THEIR RIVALS/ENEMIES

This group of epithets presents the picture of dominant person pitted against a weak adversary. These adversaries are often described as people with physical abilities, or as birds of carrion. This is demeaning to political rivals of the patron. Fighting this kind of image usually results in conflict. Praise names in this category include,

Naa Dimani:

1. Dimani barila bandi, ka o nyɛli Yɛnkana kpahiri buɣula.

Dimani shackles shackles, and his sibling Yɛnkana beats bells.

(Dimani shackles (people) while his brother Yɛnkana rings a bell.)

Dimani captures slaves while his brother sends them to the auction.

Yɛlizɔli lana Gurumanchaɣu:

2. Tɔri' ŋmaan' ʒee ni yirigi nɔhi.

Kite-dove red will stir chickens.

The red kite will cause a stir among the chickens.

Naa Zanjina:

3. Suligbaŋ nya wɔb laa zoli m balisi balisi gbe mɔɣuni.

Hawk see elephant male afterbirth stalk-stalk sleep bush.

(A flock of hawks have struggled in vain to eat an elephant's afterbirth.)

No ethnic group can match my Kingdom.

Kumpati ku ŋubi sabili:

4. Laringa yi tabi pia zuɣu, jaambɔna awei ni siɣisi o na.

Squirrel if perch platform on, clubs nine will bring-down him here.

A club will bring down the squirrel perching on a height.

5. Tandɔɣu lɔŋ kum bɔli saa, saa mi ni bu o.

Quarry-trench frog cry call rain, rain too will thrash him.

The frog in the creek has dared rain; rain will thrash him.

Naa Andan Siʋili:

6. Ba, she ŋun nye o (karimbaan) bindi ni va o karimbaan bindi.

Dog type who defecate his impudence feces will pick up his impudent feces.

The dog who impudently defecates at a prohibited place will clean up its feces.

7. Pupɔrigu zaŋ gbuʋinli bini wɔlim wɔlim je, n naan labisi ti sɔŋ gbuʋinli dooshee.

Spotted-one take lion property struggle in-vain, then return to put-down lion resting-place.

The leopard has returned the lion's property to the lion's den after toiling in vain with it.

Naa Saa lan Ziblim:

8. Din ni niŋ din niŋ ka paʋ' bia niŋ maai, din ni chɛ din che ka paʋ bia niŋ maai.

What will happen should happen and woman son body cool, what will cease should cease and woman son body cool

(Whatever is to come should come and let man be free.)

I am not afraid of all your machinations.

Naa Yaakubu Nantoo:

9. O pala piɛri nantoo, o pala niʋi nantoo, o nyɛla Dagbaŋ zaa nabihi nantoo, nabia yi ti niŋ parapiito, Yaakuba ŋun gbaagi o.

He is neither a sheep-anthrax nor a cattle-anthrax: he is anthrax to Dagbon's princes, so that he captures any prince who dares him.

Naa Alhassan (Katini) Tipariga:

10. Ʒiim taai kuliga/kurugu, ka chichɛnsi wɔlim je.

Blood consume river/metal, and mice struggle tire.

The river/metal is all bloodied and vermin struggle in vain (they cannot eat it).

Naa Mahama Kpema.

11. Bin' suŋ yoli daa ku kɔŋ dara.

Thing good late-arrive market won't lack buyer

A good product will always sell no matter how late it arrives at the market.

Gbuluŋ lana Yinifa:

12. Yɔʋuni gbuʋuma laʋim kɔbiga ku gbaai Binbiɛm shɛnli.

Bush lions number hundred won't catch Binbiɛm porcupine
A hundred lions cannot catch the Porcupine from Kumbuŋ

N.B.: A quick note here on the double edgedness of proverbial language.
In Dagbon it is the overlord, the Yaa Naa who is referred to as the lion. By this
choice, Yinifa has shot himself in the foot, and risks losing the opportunity to
rise to a higher title like Kumbungu. This name-choice will be regarded as
sauciness.

Mahami Akonsi (Nimpabɔni):
13. Bɛ ʒin zaŋ doo nini baŋ doo, faashee doo tuma ni.
They never take man face know man, except man deeds in.
A man is remembered for his deeds not his good looks

Savilugu naa Mahama Piɛvu (Zin'yarigu):
14. Zinyarigu tooi yaara, o kutooi yaa Sallama dapala, kurugu duvu.
kingfisher able remove, he cannot remove Sallama son metal pot.
The kingfisher preys over fish but not over Sallama's son, the iron pot.

Savilugu (Tugu) lana Iddi:
15. Bɛ bi zuhi ma ka n timda n tɔli.
They not invite me but I dip in my own.
They have not invited me, but I will gate-crash.

Kar' naa Alhassan Somɔa:
16. Somɔa ku zo ka chɛ o ba tiŋa.
Somɔa will not flee and leave his father town.
Somɔa will not flee from the danger in his home.

Yɛlizoli lana Asimaan Chuvu:
*17. Kɔŋ' n nya o data n vuri kpub kpub, ka vuri tɔbu, amii o leei yɛn
tɔmi bee o yɛn labi mi?*
Leper see his rival and crawl and drag bow, I-wonder he will shoot or he
will throw?
A leper has seen his rival and begins to drag a bow. Is he is going to hurl
the bow at him, or can he shoot a bow and arrow?

*18. Zin-nyɛri nya shavu zuvu n doli turi mɔva, ka Yɔvu kpamba suhuri
Naawuni tiri sa'wuu zanibu dali, ka biɛŋ kom ti nyuui ka che mɔva kom;*

ka zin-nyɛri yɛn ʒini tarigi ʒinibu, ka kuli vuri pali pali ka vuri yuli, ka ʒi' suŋ leei goo n ŋmaligi kuhi o.

(A cripple sees the flooded creek and insults the distant river. We await the dry season, to see where he will drink from.)

Do not cut off the hand that feeds you.

Yɛlizoli lana Yidaantɔvima:

19. Dini m beni? Shɛli n kani.

What be-there? Something not-there.

What's there to fear? There's nothing to be afraid of.

Banvim lana Mahama Kookali:

20. N yi kuli bi so so amaa n so Kpataribo naa nim bana.

I if just not better-than anyone but I better-than Kpataribo naa folk them.

At least I am better than the chief of Kpataribɔvu.

Kumbun naa Zakali:

21. Kandinim dabari zaana Kɔro.

Kandi-folk deserted-compounds institutor, Kɔro.

Koro, the annihilator of Kandi folk.

22. Zakali daa ŋmanila zunzuuli bindi kɔbiri Kpɛvu dali, ka ŋmani buv'nooŋa kum bɔli tindaamba, ka ŋmani wanzam n pindi o taba (bihi) zuvuri.

Zakali was like a hairy caterpillar during the Kpɛvu battle, and like a sacred bird that calls the priests, and like a barber who shaves his peers (i.e. beheads them).

Chɔvu naa Nayi:

23. Nyina lana (kunduŋ) che kɔbili yɛla, laanban sala lana (yiŋ baa) di mali karimbaani.

Teeth owner (hyena) leave bone matter, gum slippery owner (domestic dog) shouldn't have impudence.

The dog should not pretend he can break a bone the hyena has abandoned.

Kasuli lana Yahaya:

24. Soonga ŋun ŋmɛlim ku gbaai baa.

Rabbit who grow-fat won't catch dog.

No matter its size, a rabbit cannot catch a dog.

PRAISE NAMES THAT DESCRIBE RIVALS AS COUNTERFEIT

In the following example, Luro intimates he is the only legitimate heir to the throne. All other princes are illegitimate.

> Naa Luro:
> Ba' luli (baa) bi ŋmani ba' dariga/ piiriga: Paɣ' tiro bi ŋmani paɣ' faro.
> Dog-litter dog not be-like dog-bought: Wife-given not be-like wife-snatched.
> A home-raised dog is unlike one that is bought: A legal wife is unlike an illegal one.

PRAISE NAMES THAT CELEBRATE ARROGANCE/DEFIANCE

Epithets in this category encourage patrons to break the norm, and attain the high office of nam "royalty", irrespective of what the cost is, to them or to others. And once that goal has been achieved, they should be prepared to die rather than flee. One such example is this one os Somɔa,

> Kar' naa Alhassan Somɔa:
> Somɔa ku zo ka chɛ o ba tiŋa.
> Somɔa will not flee and leave his father town.
> Somɔa will not flee from the danger in his home.

Among the negative praise names twenty four of them (33, 46, 61, 64, 69, 71-79, 81, 85-90, 92-94) cast insinuations, twenty two (34, 37, 42-46, 51, 53-55, 58, 65, 67-69, 71, 75, 79, 82, 85, 87) describe others in derogatory terms, while twenty four describe their bearer as mightier than others (35, 39, 41, 43, 44, 46, 49, 50, 52, 53, 56, 57, 59, 60, 63, 66, 67, 68, 70, 80, 83, 84, 94, 95), one says a counterfeited thing cannot be like the original (36), three talk of people transgressing their bounds (38, 40, 62), one asks its bearer to appropriate what is good for oneself, damn the consequences (48), while another one asks its bearer to be unaccommodating (62).

Some names, like the last one (Kar' naa Alhassan Somɔ a's), however, are multi-dimensional, and could be given both positive and negative interpretations.

Somɔa ku zo ka che o ba tiŋa
Somɔa Not run and leave his father town.
Somɔa will not flee from his fatherland in the face of danger.

In a positive vein, this epithet encourages courage and patriotism. This compares with what Paredes (1994: 33) writes of the Gregorio Cortez, when the hero says "I will break before I bend." Like Cortez, Somɔa is a 'man' and would rather die than flee from the land of his birth. Its negative dimension is that, Somɔa's action was an exhibition of sauciness and disrespect for authority. He dared rebel against his superior, Naa Andani Jengbariga. This arrogant and unbending character prevented Somɔa from fleeing when Naa Andani came to attack him. If he had left the scene the bloodbath that led to his death would have been averted. There is mutual hatred between their descendants today.

In this category of negative names we see descriptions of rivals as arrogant, dirty and destructive vermin, locusts, cowardly monkeys, and wicked witches, among others. Enemies have physical deformities, are fools, have oblong heads and rotten mouths. Naa Andani Zɔli chooses the praise epithet "tɔli kami ka sakɔʋu be "A locust and a grasshopper are one and the same", when he is at peace with his brothers and cousins. He is passed over for the skin, and his drummers and followers turn the name around, to tɔli bini ka sakɔʋu kpuʋi "the grasshopper has appropriated what belongs to the locust", to allude to the situation, where he has been wrongfully denied what is his. This is targeted language, and has a drum accompaniment.

In the wake of Ghana's independence from Britain, the atikatika[6] tune kpara ni jansi bɛ ŋmani taba "Gorillas and monkeys, they have a lot in common" was reinterpreted by opponents of the President, who use it to lampoon the present regime, to the effect that this regime and that of the colonialist British are alike in all ways.

CONCLUSION

Praise names that call on the patron to emulate the good works or habits of their forebears will be tagged positive names, and those that lampoon, cast insinuations, or incense others are those that I have classified as negative

---

[6] This is a recreational dance form for the youth. They use songs that could be profane, or lampoon others.

names. Those names that portray patrons as primus inter pares are not negative if they do not dress them in borrowed garbs, that is, portray them as who they are not. A name that boosts the ego and motivates one to achieve higher laurels is, to say the least, a positive name, and those that ill-advise the patron are negative.

Chapter 6

AT SAMBAN LUŊA: A COMPOSITE PRAISE SINGING SESSION

> It is for the people of tomorrow's sake that our forebears
> instituted the drummer institution, so that whoever listens
> to them today, shall be wiser and have a better tomorrow.
> A popular saying of drummers.

I find this excerpt from Connerton (2007: 2) fitting to open this chapter, which deals with how Dagomba society remembers its past. He notes that,

> Our experience of the present very largely depends upon our
> knowledge of the past. We experience our present world in a
> context which is causally connected with past events and objects,
> and hence with reference to events and objects which we are not
> experiencing when we are experiencing the present. And we will
> experience our present differently in accordance with the different
> pasts to which we are able to connect that present.

Historiography, the writing down of history in the modern sense, is a new phenomenon in Africa, where the oral tradition has been the main source of the peoples' histories. Oral historians of today have come to respect the oral traditions of Africa; especially the epic songs sung, as a primary source of the African past, even if the paradigms used may not strictly be factual (see Belcher 1999: 5). Epics, as defined by Biebuyck (1978: 336), "... are long, orally transmitted poetic narratives presented in an episodic manner and intermittently." In Western scholarship on the epic, Homer's *Iliad* and the *Odyssey* occupy a prominent position. Also important among scholars of literature and folklore are the epic traditions of the Serbo-Croats of Yugoslavia (Southeastern Europe and the Balkans, especially Serbia and Montenegro), India (see Honko), and the Finnish Kalevala.

African societies rely extensively on this genre of narrative poetry, where practitioners use elevated language to tell or recount the histories of legendary traditional heroes. In this verbal genre, where the language used is akin to that of a cultural in-group usage, each performer, praise singer or patron, chooses words that will captivate the audience and influence them to act in a certain way. McDowell (2000: 24-25) expresses this same view, that,

> The aesthetic concern is to create a narrative that captivates
> its audience by virtue of enticing formal structures and arresting
> formulations of themes, . . . a mode of signification characterized
> by stylized discourse.

This principle not only directs the speaker-performer's diction, it also helps shape the entire speech event to suit the situation. This is evidenced by the frequent digressions, comments and occasion praise within a praise session. Women ululate and call out praises of the both griot and patron when they feel the musician is in the groove, and doing a good job of the narration/performance. This further motivates the artist to give of his best. Ululalors are also rewarded monetarily by the personalities they assist in praising.

Belcher[1] categorizes African epics into three broad groups, on the basis of geography, content and performance features. The first group, from Northern Africa, are adaptations of Arabic epic traditions of the *Bani Hilal* cycle, and the Swahili *Utenzi*, some of which are translations from Arabic texts, along the east coast; the second group, from Central Africa, involves cycles which are more mythical than historical (e.g., *Mwindo* of BaNyanga, *Lianja* of Mondo, *Ozidi* of the Ijo, Swahili *Liyongo*, Zulu *Hlakanyaka*, Malagasy *Ibonia*). Their heroes possess extraordinary magical powers. The third group are those of West Africa, where the songs draw upon a historical base and delineate characters who have had tremendous impacts on their times. Joyce (2004: 115) notes that,

> The history of the entire area is marked by the building of great
> centralized empires whose internal organization was based on a

---

[1] See Introduction to Stephen Belcher 1999.

hierarchical class system in which each saw his place assigned
by his birthright, status and social function.

In this light epics encompass some legendary power struggle. John
William Johnson (1999: 12) also observes this as a major characteristic of the
West African epic. Important examples of epic battles are those involving Son-
Jara and Sumamuru (Mandinka), Zanjina/Andaan Sivili and Goliŋgoliŋ
Kumpati, Luro and Dajia (Dagomba).

Praise poetry in Africa encompasses both panegyrics and epics. Belcher
(1999: 16) notes that,

> Clan or lineage poems and songs of praise necessarily evoke clan
> history and the celebrated individuals of the past. The praise song may
> sometimes tell a story, as would an epic, although allusion and indirect
> reference are the typical tropes of panegyric. Further, praise songs are
> incorporated into epics in varying degrees, and they appear inextricable
> from certain aspects of the epic performance.

In their effort to recollect the past events, past and present factors struggle
to either influence or distort each other, hence the drummers take this
performance session very seriously, and seek "divine" intervention to carry out
their task of presenting a "true" narrative. H. A. Blair[2], the colonial British
Commissioner for Eastern Dagomba realized just how aatached the Dagomba
people were attached to their drum histories when the colonial administration
met with the local folk to draw a constitution for Dagbon. In his commentary
he notes that,

> It is a general rule, that amongst people whose sole knowledge of their
> origins consists of a succession of legends of heroic deed performed by
> their leaders, these leaders and their wanderings and deeds represent
> tribes
> and their movements.

He also alludes to the patriarchal legends of the Old Testament to support
this thesis that the heroes' histories are representative of their peoples' history.
Samban luŋa "Courtyard Drumming" is the quintessence of drum lore, an

---

[2] See A. Duncan-Johnstone 1930.

occasion during which the drummer is put to the ultimate test when he is asked to lead the whole ensemble in decanting epic poetry.

Belcher (2004: 113-4) observes that the epic performance tradition as found across Africa often incorporates music and deals with historical narratives with subjects that involve myths, legends of origin, or recent historical anecdotes of local heroes. However, unlike the epics from the Sahelian region which have lost ". . . much of their historical weight and develop[ed] along purely narrative and artistic lines", the Dagomba epic places equal premium on history and artistry. They emcompass the political and cultural history of the communities in which they are told (see Okpewho 1992: 202).

This session has three episodes: *ʒiɛri tɔbu* 'preparation', *nam balimbu* 'seeking permission', and *mɔni* 'the main meal'. All the praise types are brought together at this session, and this is what we are going to examine in this chapter. I have observed in a review of Finnegan (2007)[3] that "Written literature may have an independent and tangible existence, but it is the live, oral version that has the enviable aspect of being performed; the event giving the performance its shape and texture. On-going improvisation, clarifications and challenges from the audience enrich the oral performance." This is a perfect description of what goes on in a typical epic rendition session, where the bard structures his poem as the performance event unfolds. He intersperses his song with praises directed to the patron at whose house the session is taking place, welcomes and goodbyes dignitaries as they come and go, comments on events, past and present; and depending on audience reception the performance may last the whole night or a part thereof[4]. A solo drum punctuates the rhythm for the narrating griot, and after each line he sings there is an answering drum chorus. The text I present here is thus stripped of a greater part of its oral garb, largely because I have been looking out for a specific ingredient, the praise name. The messages communicated on the drummer's speaking drums for example, are not captured here.

---

[3] See Abdulai Salifu's review of March 26, 2008 at http://www.indiana.edu/~jofr/reviews.php.
[4] During the performance the lead drummer spent so much time at the preparatory stage to remember departed ancestors, and at a point was told by one of his team-mates that it was past midnight; meaning they needed to speed up their narration.

THE SAMBAN' LUNA SESSION

Drummers gather in the forecourt of the chief in the evening of the eve of major Dagomba festivals to sing the histories of legendary eminent personalities. The histories that surround these personalities, who are are past Kings of the ethnic group, are by and large the history of the Dagomba nation (as noted by H.A. Blair above). This is what gives epic its preeminent position in Dagomba praise poetry. It is panegyric and historic narrative combined.

When they arrive at the performance scene they kick-start the evening of performance with a preliminary stage (known as *ʒiɛri tɔbu*), that they liken to processing ingredients for the preparation of a meal. During this stage the lead drummer leads the ensemble in an invocation of a sort, and moves on to a second stage where they seek permission from the chief to engage in their enterprise (*nam balimbu*), and finally delve into the third and final stage, the main story they have to tell (*mɔni*). This metaphor/image of preparing for, and eventually cooking, a meal for a spouse is important in defining the roles of drummer and patron. It speaks of the functional 'husband-wife' relationship between them.

1. *Ʒiɛri Tɔbu* "Processing the Soup Ingredients"

In this opening to the performance event, the poet recounts genealogies of drummer-ancestors whose blessings and protection he seeks for the present performance. As he recounts their histories he reconstructs the family tree, showing the relationship between the kings and drummers, and also invokes the spirits of these ancestors and the drum spirits (the instrument has a soul of its own) telling them the night is for them. He challenges them to enable the performers have a "good performance", for failure is unbefitting of them. As he enumerates these ancestors he salutes them with their praise epithets as well. The singer opens with the call,

> Yɛtɔγa yɛlimi ka n deei n bɔhim yɛligu.
> Speech speak and I take-over learn speech
> Spirit of Oratory, speak so that I may learn to speak.

> N yaba pami ma zim ka m moni
> My grandfather put-on me flour and I stir.
> Add flour into the cooking pot while I stir it up.

That is to say, his grandfather should take control of the situation, for, he as a 'mere child' cannot handle it unassisted. This echoes Richard Bauman's (1978/1984: 20) disclaimer of performance, so that while elevating the dead relations the living drummer simultaneously shows his humility, when he ascribes all that is aesthetic to ancestors, a deference to these virtuosic forebears. The staple diet of the Dagomba is a corn/sorghum meal stirred up into a paste and eaten with soup. This is the meal a bard asks to be assisted to cook. He evokes this image to show the functional marital relationship between the artist and his patron. The artist has come to perform the wifely duty of cooking for the husband, as is the Dagomba custom. He invokes the spirits of his ancestors to see him through the narration, and enumerates them and calls their praise epithets as well. In uttering the words *yɛligu* 'Oratory/ speech' the drummer, like the *oriki* performer Karin Barber (1991: 249) talks of, accesses the narrative corpus as well as opens the channels of communication between the living and the dead.

2. *Na' Balima* "Prelude to Narration Of Epic"

At this point in the narration the drummers change tempo and rhythm, signaling that another high point has been reached, a stage where they not only acknowledge their benefactor, but also seek permission to proceed with their assignment. The lead singer asks the king to come out and supplicate for God's intercession, so that the nation will be peaceful and prosperous. During this whole process, the drummer poet's artistic abilities are put to the utmost test as he selects his materials for the main performance. He is both creating and recreating history, for his performance will itself be a historic product which will be referred to for several generations to come, whether for its artistic quality or its mediocrity. As the recitation of genealogies continues into the late hours of the night the drummers urge their husband to come out. When he eventually does so, they plead with him to tread cautiously for earthly calm, and then finally, he should sit calmly, as can be found in Appendix 6, page 133,

> I beseech you!
> I ask for permission!! [stylistic element]
> Slowly, carefully, owner of the earth, your mercies, please.
> The one who owns all, tread softly for calmness on earth.
> King of the rear and the fore, tread softly for calm on earth

Earthly intercessor

The episode foregrounds the importance of the drummer as one who persuades the powerful, to balance their power with mercy. Their use of the archaic word *Nyɔvilo*[5] further drives home their seriousness, conjuring archaisms to present their material using imperatives. They ask the king to listen attentively, as found in,

> Son of one who exits through-the-broken-wall[6],
> open your ears and hear matters of your father's house.

When a king dies the wall near the entrance hallway is pushed down, and his corpse is taken out of the palace via the gaping hole in the wall, to the burial room (Katini) in an adjoining house. The wives are expected to exit through the same passage, if they have been faithful. Any wife who had extra marital relations while the king was alive will die if she exits through this last route the deceased king took to leave this house. The king's wives are thus referred to as those who exit via the pushed down wall. The patron is here being told he is not born of a 'common' woman, but of one who is not only royal but passes the test of loyalty to husband.

In the prelude to the epic poetry rendition, the bard brings all forms of praises together. He uses biological names, terms of endearment, titles, as well as praise epithets as props for the spectacle he is creating. The more theatrical his performance is, the more favorably he will be evaluated by his audience. There is some historical element in this genealogy narrated in this prelude to the high point of the performance, but this is not the 'true' epic, as noted by Okpewho (1999: 202), who calls it a heroic narrative, where the singer may give his narration a partisan slant. This is not so with the main epic.

When the king takes his seat, they move to the third stage, the singing of the epic. The most popular of the songs is the one of the 18th King, Zanjina, son of Timtituyuri, who is the most innovative of all the Yaa Naas.

---

[5] Nyɔvilo is an archaic form, only used in poetry today. Its colloquial cognate is fabila "complaints/ pleas/ beseeching."

[6] The wives of the deceased are expected to exit through the samebroken fence wall, if they have been faithful. Any wife who had extra marital relations while the king was alive will die if she exits through this last route the deceased king took to leave this house. The king's wives are thus referred to as those who exit via the pushed down wall.

3. The Legendary Naa Zanjina

Introduction

The Dagomba king Zanjina is the most popular, because of the innovations he brought into the people's ways. His reign saw many innovations, thus making him the first choice for epic song.

The Zanjina story is more than a mere tale, or historical narrative. It is a big metaphor of the life of the Dagbon nation, and there are many lessons to be derived therefrom. I listened to this reproduction of the poem from my primary drummer informant, and for ease of narration I have decided to detach the praise names from the personages, and attach them in an appendix. It is characteristic to juxtapose people's biological names with their praise epithets whenever they are mentioned in the course of the narration. Narrators will occasionally use the praise epithet in place of a person's birth name.

The Story

The story goes that, Zanjina's mother, affectionately called Daughter of Ŋmayaɣisi Koomba was from Sankuni, that is, Sabali (Bimbarigu)[7]. Naa Luro's oldest son, Timtituɣuri, contrary to everyone's expectations, marries ugly Adisa 'Nanga' from Sabali. She is called Nanga because of her ugly outlook. When the husband ascends to the Yani skin (throne), the elders tell her that they have elevated her to a higher status in a statement, *ti ti a yuli* "we have given you a name", which later gets nominalized into what is now known in the hierarchy of Yaa Naa's wives as Napaɣ *Taayili* 'King's wife Taayili'. The import of the name "We have given you a name" is that, they of the royal household have taken a lowly placed and not-so-good-looking person; and elevated her to a position of prominence. She is now a titled person, one befitting none other than the King himself. Napaɣ Taayili first gives birth to a girl, Nana Maliyam (naa Maliyam), before giving birth to Bɔligu Lana (also Boliŋ lana) Zanjina in her second birth. When the then king, naa Gungɔbili, dies Zanjina is in the Krachi area gambling. He comes home, and his sister advises him to go and salute Kuɣu naa Gban Nyoma Biɛŋ [Praise name 1][8], and other older princes – Yɛlizɔli lana Gurumanchaɣu [Praise name 8], Nakuŋ

---

[7] A mother's place of birth is as important in a person's praise names as the name one chooses for oneself.

[8] For ease of narration, I shall attach the numerals 1, 2, 3, etc, after the name of personages mentioned. The praise epithets are listed in Table 6.1.

lana Wun'yuʋuri [10], Laligbaŋ lana Zanjin' Ʒɛʋu [11], Worivi lana Mo'nyoo [12], Kpuʋuli lana Binyahim [15], Gundowuʋiri lana Kushiwoo [14], Zaʋili dapala Andaan' Siʋili [41]. She also hints to him that their forebears once told her that if the sons of the same father contest for the *nam* that is the beginning of the crumbling of the kingdom, and that in this likely event there will be the need for an intercession by the King of Ɔmampurugu, who is historically the Dagomba King's older brother. Zanjina should therefore go and solicit his friendship, knowing that the princes would eventually come to the Ɔmapurugu King (the Nayiri) for a selection from amongst them. Information reaches his rivals that Zanjina had gone to the Nayiri to canvas the namship, so they, the other competitors decide that they would go there also.

Kuʋu naa [1], who is the eldest, does not travel abroad and so delegates Gushe' naa Kpeem'biɛʋu [2], and Buŋ Ti'kurugu [4] to go with these princes to the Nayiri's court for arbitration. History has it that the great ancestors of the four major ethnic groups of Northern Ghana put in place a mechanism whereby if matters ever got to a head in the affairs of Dagbaŋ the Nayiri would resolve it and the Yaa Naa would do same if Ɔmampurugu found itself in crises. Nanuŋ and Zabaʋu (Gonjaland) were similarly matched for mutual resolution of crises.

When the party gets to Kariga Gunaayili, the chief, Gu' naa Azima asks them if Kuʋu naa had informed them of *Yoʋu Sochira* "Dagbaŋ's crossroads, at Baʋili[9], and the Gbangbantua in Ɔmampurugu."[10] It is taboo for royals from the two kingdoms to ever set eyes on these towns. The symbolism here is that those two are the farthest spots in the respective kingdoms, so if a prince who still aspires to a higher title sees those towns he is deemed to have reached his peak of achievement, and would thus no longer make any progress. Buŋ Tikurugu [4] goes back to Kuʋu naa, who confirms what Gunaa said. He tells Tikurugu in Dagbani that *Yoʋu sochira zooya ŋmampurugu soli* "Dagbaŋ's crossroads are numerous on the way Ɔmampirigu, meaning, there are many obstacles enroute to Ɔmampirugu". They cross the Kariga River, Go-n-kpe-nyoŋ-ni "travel into the the forest.", and meet Falinga, a Mampurusi royal who had been cast out from his hometown, and was running away to Dagbaŋ. He,

---

[9] "Baʋili saani" "Stranger to Baʋili" is one of the Yaa Naa's praises, referencing the fact that that land must always be 'strange land' to him. His soul resides there after he has passed.

[10] The luŋa, as the keeper of public records, also keeps track of land borders, and my informant here gives the boundaries between the two Kingdoms of Dagbaŋ and Ɔmampurugu.

an indigene, is erroneously now being referred to as *zino* 'stranger'. The Dagomba royals then tell him they were also in a similar crisis situation, to which he replied in the local parlance,

> Din dina ti yɛla la miiya: di miiya zaa gamgam It then our matters FOC
> be-sour: it be-sour completely Ideophone
> In that case this situation of ours is really critical'.

This exchange gives the town the new name Dimiigi (literally, "It has turned sour"), and they make Falinga chief, with the title Dimiigi Lana Zino [5]. They bypass Tundi, but are made to return by the chief of Tundi, Yirigim Bamba [7], who tells them the Nayiri is away, at the funeral of the Nakpanzɔŋ earth priest, whom the Nayiri claimed was his maternal uncle, ostensibly because the deceased was wealthy. Yirigi Bamba then sends an emissary to inform the Nayiri of the guests he is entertaining. After inheriting property of the late Nakpanzɔŋ Tindana (without accepting the shrine and responsibilities that go with it), the Nayiri returns home to meet his guests.

While enroute to the Nayiri's palace Bɔligu lana Zanjina asks his head drummer to turn his drum upside down; so that as the other contestants went in pomp, his retinue was silent. At the instance of the Mamprusi King the elders of Mampurugu are asked to choose a King from among the field of princes. They fail to come to a consensus, much to the annoyance of the King who rebukes them, telling them that it was disunity, and dissonant voices that had led to the predicament in which his 'brothers' now found themselves, and he was disappointed his elders were behaving likewise. He decides he will make the choice himself.

At the assembly he asks the contestants to take turns to tell the gathering what their respective praise names are, so that the person who has the wittiest epithet will be the Dagomba King. Kpeem'biɛvu being the most senior is asked to begin. Tundi Lana objects, and challenges the Gushe' naa to a contest in proverb lore, because their towns occupy identical outpost positions in their respective kingdoms; plus they had also previously quarreled at sharing booty during one of their exploits. The Tundi lana chooses names that allude to the greed and avarice of Kpeem'biɛvu who speechlessly leaves the durbar grounds for his host's house. The latter's grandson is surprised to find the old man at home when the party he had brought to Ŋmampirigu is still at the Nayiri's house. Upon inquiry the reluctant grandfather tells the young man his reason for leaving the assembly. This young man [3] tells the old man to go back and reply Tundi Lana's taunts with the names as listed in the table under

Kpeenbiɛvu. After receiving this advice, Kpeem'biɛvu asks Naatili Lana, Zantili lana, and Yitiligi lana, (his elders) to go and behead the grandson, lest he reveals that it was him that gave him (Kpeenbiɛvu) the words to reply Tundi lana with. Before dying the youth in his dying words tells the Kpeenbiɛvu:

> A yi ku ma a ni paŋ mɔri.
> You if kill me you will borrow hay.
> If you kill me you shall miss my services.
>
> M maliya ka kuni n kɔŋko, bili' chavu ni
> I repair and go-home alone, fountain dry in.
> (I now end up in a dried up well after my good service to you.)
> I am unjustly rewarded for my good services.
>
> Yɛl' baŋdi kunila o kɔŋko.
> Matter knower goes-home him alone.
> The puzzle solver travels alone (gets killed).

Contestant after contestant rises to give their praise names (see Table below), but the Nayiri finds fault with them all, and uses that to disqualify them for the *nam*. Andaan Sivili [41], who rises before Boligu lana Zanjina, realizes the Nayiri's design and chooses names that clearly indicate his anger and displeasure. Zanjina calls his names last, which the Nayiri declares the best, and names befitting a Yaa Naa; and hence declares him winner.

These are praise epithets detached from the narration of the Naa Zanjina epic in order to facilitate narration. These personalities have come to have their praise names shortened into becoming their "actual" names.

Personalities and their Praise Names

1. Kuv' naa Gban' Nyɔma Biɛŋ
    - One cannot tell which one of the frogs croaking in the creek is older.
    - The good farm that is close to the marsh land shall produce early yam tubers.
2. Gushe' naa Kpeem'Biɛvu
    - One should correct oneself if one cannot correct a bad elder.

- The evening partridge has tricked the tree and slept on the ground; and also conspires to unearth the farmer's recently planted grain.
- The sorghum has not germinated; the flock of birds should come and toil in vain. (responce to Tundi lana's taunt)

3. Kpeem'Bieɣu's Grandson who gave him the wise words to retaliate Tundi lana's taunts)
   - The wicked wealthy person conspires to destroy a poor man's farm.
   - The bowl of porridge demeans the spoon and the spoon has finished him.
   - Do not underestimate the wisdom of the young.

4. Buŋ' Ti'kurigu
   - The rooster's bribe will not protect him from the hawk.

5. Dimii' lana Zino
   - Supposedly dry woods have surprised gatherers of faggots by growing new leaves.

6. Yinfa = Dimiigi Lana's son.
   - The snake has gotten onto slippery terrain its speed has deteriorated.

7. Tundi lana Yirigim Bamba
   - A flock of birds will swoop on millet grains.
   - The foolish elder who goes into the millet farm.
   - We do not rub our butts when the fire fly sticks to them.
   - Fire shall annihilate all the grass.
   - When the foolish elder eats greasy food let us wait for the day matters of the tummy will arise.

8. Yɛlizɔli lana Gurumanchaɣu
   - The red kite will cause a stir among the fowls.
   - Too much filing destroys the metal.
   - The crossroads have wickedly led the stranger astray.

9. Sunsɔŋ lana Timani
   - Necessity makes people lie on a bedbug infested mat.
   - You misbehave because you are untouchable (you are well-connected).

10. Nakuŋ lana Wun' yuɣuri
    - The cat's bag is unacceptable here.
    - Do not postpone important matters to a later date.

11. Laligbaŋ lana Zanjin' Ȝiɛɤu
   - The old spear grass is not related to the sesame plant.
   - A single yam tuber has rendered the fufu unwholesome. = one bad nut destroys the whole bunch.

12. Wɔrivi lana Mo' nyoo
   - I, Mo' nyoo, cannot be grounded.
   - Spear grass says that the farmer who messes around him will get scarred.

13. Andan' Siɤili, son of Zaɤili.
   - It is love that keeps the family together.
   - The Conqueror. One who fights for the King does not need to publicize himself.
   - Struggles shall clear the ground. Nothing happens in without a cause.
   - The lion's roar shall cause a stir in the town.
   - Scattered grains of millet shall assemble chickens.
   - The blessed foundry shall assemble metals.
   - It is impossible to know the contents of a whole egg.
   - The dog who defecates at a prohibited place will clean up its feces.
   - Sounding the lunatic's drum will ignite the town: One does not incense a lunatic.
   - Too much suspicion/segregation will lead to whole scale distrust of people around you.
   - A family needs to be united in order to escape the world's evil/hatred. (A united front overcomes all malice).
   - A huge pot that cannot pass through the doorway is hauled in across the wall.

14. Gundowuɤiri lana Kushiwoo
   - Like old trees, when old royals are near death they develop numerous ailments/complaints.
   - Magnificent Kushiwoo, the indomitable.

15. Kpuɤili lana Binyahim
   - A plush thorny tree will be an ideal resting spot, but stumps will not make that possible.
   - The hungry looking goat will endure wet season hardship.

16. Zanjina

- The broad chest shall accommodate a lot of adornments.
- It is difficult to know which silkcotton fruit on the kapok tree is older.
- A flock of hawks have struggled in vain to eat an elephant's afterbirth. [To wit, if he becomes King rival ethnic groups will not be able to match his Kingdom.]
- A greedy king inherits the property of the deceased, but not the responsibility that goes with it.
- A diseased kola nut is best discarded.
- The child with clean hands that skins the elders' goat. Even though he eats all but the stomach and the liver, the elder does not get mad with him.
- One cannot distinguish between baby and afterbirth.
- Unbreakable Meteorite of the Akɔɣu battle
- Wars shall harm neither Dagbaŋ nor Ŋmampirigu.

17. Ŋmampirigu Tɔbilaan Kpɛma (army commander)
   - Use the right route to have access to what you want.
   - The tongue is the route to one's inner essence.
   - To be set up is more painful than being impaled by a spear.
   - (he went to confer with the Nayiri, and to advise him on the method to use in choosing a Yaa Naa)

18. Kpinkpanzɔŋ lana Tumba (Nayiri's head drummer)
   - The young shall grow.

19. Ŋmampirigu Lana Wɔbigu = Naa Tampuli's grandfather
   - A good elephant stands beside a shed (He does not destroy it).

20. Ŋmampirigu Lana Tampuli
   - It is only a fool who says there is no God. Death will teach them that God is alive.

21. Ŋmampirigu Lana Shɛri Kpɛma
   - He is the one who unites both Dagbon and Ŋmampirigu.

22. Ŋmampirigu naa Dawura
   - Chickens are restless because hawk has made its nest on a palm tree close to the house.
   - The fool who is not cautioned continues to be abusive.
   - They brag because they have been given false promises.

23. Ŋmampirigu Lana Sulemani

24. Ŋmampirigu Lana Ziblim

- They mock others' children, and won't mock theirs.

25. Ŋmampirigu Lana Tampuli
   - Being set up is worse than being impaled.
   - The humble one successfully builds houses, but the proud one dies before his house is completed.

26. Kamshaᵧu Lana Amadu
   - Dimbu is (I am) self sufficient.

27. Gaa Tuuviɛligu Naa
   - The leper has perennial sore toe.

28. Gushaᵧu Lunnaa, Darikɔᵧu naa Kachaᵧu
   - One who is an excessive grabber is also a trouble rouser.
   - Excessive hunger will breed fighting.

29. Kumpati ku ŋubi sabili
   - If a squirrel rests on a high platform, nine clubs will bring it down.
   - The squirrel has called the rain; rain shall thrash it.

30. Talɔli lana Bukali (Kɔbili)
   - A slave's leg cannot stir up a storm.
   - A bone that cannot be broken is abandoned.

31. Namonaa Wɔb'laa Nyɔᵧu kun dari
   - If two persons cannot co-habit they have something up their sleeve.
   - No matter the size/weight of the basket-full of okra leaves, it can be carried.

32. Tampiuŋ lana Birichim
   - The tethered goat shall stare helplessly at the foliage it cannot reach. (he's powerless).
   - Desperate situations demand desperate measures.
   - Baobab seeds have turned powdery, bean seeds should not brag.

33. Naantɔn naa Suhu bɛri bo (Do' kuᵧu)
   - A hundred arrows cannot become a spear.
   - The ugly noises of youth ceases when they get to the arena.
   - When the leopard summons the dog he means to kill the latter.
   - The soup pot shall not suffice some.
   - The Hausa donkey carries heavy loads but cannot offload them by itself.

34. ʒaŋ Mbanaa Laᵧ'chee

- There is always an evil person in even the smallest village.
- House ware cannot reject a cockroach.
- A lizard has bitten a snake; only the wise know it.
- An ulcerous sore disfigures the shin.
- It is salt that aids broth.
- The male monkey tucks in his own tail.
- Whoever confines the hyena must free it.
- Who leaves the world without their children suffering?
- When it rains we will distinguish between okra and cotton seedlings.

35. Lingbuŋ lana Dasana
    - I am the old pot that feeds the ungrateful and abusive fellow citizens.

36. Tɔlin naa Na'dima
    - The one whose horse feet flash with lightening speed, and his arrows fall like elephant grass (multitudinous).
    - The spear has seen me and wavers like a kite.
    - May God protect the spring, so that termites will benefit.

37. Kumbun' naa Suleman' Kpɛma
    - The bottom of a new mother never lacks for pain.
    - The knife blade has seen okra and cuts itself
    - The house has been surrounded by elephant grass
    - There is funfair everywhere!

    Guŋ Lana (Sulemana's subject)
    - The dog dares not lick the river's stone anvil.
    - The young river monkey will not sit on the ground.

38. Savilugu naa Puu samli
    - If the merchant cannot handle the hoe the farmer will do so.
    - Virtue will always triumph.

39. Zangbalin' naa Yaviri yua
    - The male guinea fowl makes a nest, but that does not mean he will lay eggs/roost
    - Shale cannot be like a clay flute.
    - Those who blow clay flutes shall have white lips.

40. Diyali lana Tisua
    - On the day the Diyali bushes will be set on fire some folk will cease to exist.

- On the day the Diyali bushes were to be set ablaze, a kite snatched a lady wearing nine waist-beads, and a gentleman with his guinea corn field, away. Even though the whole town burnt down, the Diyali log (Tisua) would not catch fire.
- The kite's war drums sound that destroys a race all on his own?

41. Andaan' Siyili
    - The huge pot does not pass through the doorway. It is passed over the wall.

42. Gushe' naa Yaakubu Kurili
    - One who over reaches oneself looks for trouble.
    - A lunatic has stirred up a bee hive onto himself and cries out loudly.

43. Yɛlizɔli lana Simaani (Chuyu)
    - God's gift is better than humans'
    - The lion's skin cannot dry up rain
    - A leper has seen his rival and begins to drag a bow. I wonder if he is going to hurl the bow at him, or if he can shoot a bow and arrow.
    - A cripple who sees the flooded creek and insults the distant river. We await the dry season, to see where he will drink from
    - One who blows air into a gourd of ashes gets blinded.

44. Naluŋ Yɛrinaa
    - It is the maiden from the city who terminates her pregnancy (not the rural one).
    - These are bad times.
    - Self discipline is the best remedy where there is no supervisor.

45. Nakpaa lana Dokurugu
    - The log's venom cannot overpower smoke.
    - What will happen has happened.
    - A scorpion has stung a lunatic and increased nonsensical talk.

46. Sabal' Yɛrinaa Yamusah
    - Kings are powerless against women, commoners should not even dare.
    - Gifts are rife in the year of bumper harvest.

47. Sabali lana Mahami
    - We will always find salt in the market.

48. Kari' naa Dakpayili
    - Heavy rains will not make a creeping plant become one that bears cobs.
    - The royal does not kowtow to everyone.
    - The royal won't sit on the floor. = He is not a commoner.

49. Zɔɣu lana Timaligu
    - One can only know what's in one's house, and not the whole world.
    - Inheriter of 'The fig stick cannot be broken easily'. You will hurt yourself if you attempt doing so.

50. Langɔɣu lana Binyahim
    - Tataburata! If you yearn for somebody else's property, you do so in vain.
    - A jealous woman's cuisine: She cooks "eat if you like." And then she hides in her room and eats, and comes out to pretend they are all alike.

51. Kpan' naa Ti'tiliga
    - 'Titiliga' shall waste thread. = labor not in vain!
    - The crossroads has a reward.
    - In the years of famine the hills need to be afraid of rain.

52. Zakpalisi lana Baakari
    - The rain that nourishes the tree is the same one that nourishes the grasses.
    - The leper has a perennial sore.

53. Saŋ lana Azima
    - No matter how big it grows a lizard is not tethered.

54. Bakpab' lana Kpaliga
    - The hard oakwood tree is best left alone, because your blow cannot hurt it.
    - If you mess around with the lazy man, he blames you for all his shortcomings.

55. Taɣinamo lana Kabiɣu Wari
    - One shall waste firewood to drive away the cold of the harmattan
    - An evening task is done quickly. = Brevity is the soul of business.

56. Saɣnarigu lana Binyaati = Naa Zɔrikuli's son
    - In these times it is only the wealthy that are right.

57. Sonaa Faamuru
    - The one who shoots the arrow is not the enemy: Whether a metal gets straightened or bent it is the blacksmith's fault. He fashioned the weapon. The blacksmith is supposedly the enemy= There are hidden enemies.

58. Yamusah = Yɛni Baɣili (Wunyaansi) lana's first son
    - All faggots produce smoke. = this means every woman has the natural feeling of jealousy.

59. Tɔŋ Lun' naa Tisua = Namo' naa Ashaɣu's first son

- The roan antelope's foot cannot be like a vagina (an imitation cannot be like the original).

After his victory at Ŋmampirigu, Zanjina sets out for home, to meet the cold shoulder of his defeated rivals. They would not even accept his offers for reconciliation. On his way home, he gets confounded and does not know the way to Sabali, where he intends to go to the mosque of the powerful Muslim cleric, Sabali Yɛrinaa Yamusah [46], for prayers. The roads become nine, and he knows not which leads to Sabali, Kulikabiriga (*Akɔɣu*), or to Baasali. When he starts to brood over this, his elders tell him that such behavior does not become the "Owner of the Universe." They ask for a white ram, which they sacrifice to the spirit of the crossroads, and the way gets clear for their party to proceed. When they arrive at Sabali they are greeted by an unusual quiet. Upon inquiry Zanjina is told the eldest son of the Muslim cleric, Sabali Yɛrinaa Yamusah, had died. Zanjina takes up the responsibility of performing all rites due the dead, by providing grain for food, a white cloth for the shroud, and also money to the drummers to mourn the deceased. This was unprecedented in the history of Dagbaŋ. He stayed there and saw to all the obsequies. It was here Zanjina instituted drumming at funerals (*kuli kumbu* "funeral crying" or "dirge singing", and *dikala* "a funeral dance-tune").

After this, emissaries are sent to Gambaga, Wa, Agbandi and Salaga to invite people to Sabali to assist in the cleric to pray to God for Naa Zanjina's Kingdom. Sabali Yɛrinaa looks into his Holy script and recommends a sacrifice of a hundred thousand and one cowries and a slave, to pray against an impending battle (*Akɔɣu tobu*). The items of sacrifice are given to Zanjina's son Jiŋli and Buŋ'Tikurigu to go and take care of the sacrifice on the other side of the Sabali river. Upon their return, on a Friday morning, the Imam opened the four doors of his mosque (these symbolize the four cardinal directions of the Dagbaŋ kingdom, which would be opened up for development), and lit seven lamps, saying he wanted Zanjina's kingdom to be as bright as the seven lamps, cool (symbol of peace) as the rainy season, and soft as clay (no hardship). Zanjina then proceeds home.

It was during his reign that people started wearing cloth, women started wearing beads (*samarimavi*), the blind were given staffs to lead them outdoors, and lepers started wearing donkey-hoof-boots. Prior to this the disabled were left indoors. It was Zanjina who gave them access to the outside world again, after their impairment/disability. He also instituted purification rites that freed widows and widowers so that they could remarry. Zanjina's prayers lit the light that would illuminate the road for merchants to find their way to market places, far and near.

When Zanjina arrives at his headquarters news reaches him of the Gonja warlord, Gɔliŋgɔliŋ Kumpati's [29] annexation of many Dagomba towns. He is told that only Andaan' Siʋili could match Kumpati, but Siʋili, who had been slighted by Zanjina at ŋmampirigu, was abroad in Chakosi land. He gets into a fight with a Chakosi man by name Andani after Siʋili had won a gambling contest against his namesake. In the impending battle of the two Andanis the Dagomba Andani slays his Chakosi rival, and is accompanied home with praises by his bard, Namonaa Wab'laa-Nyɔʋu-kun-dari [31] to Dagbaŋ, but decides to pitch camp on the outskirts, at Zulɔʋu Kpali'yɔʋu (the Zulɔʋu woods). The epic battle of the two Andani giants marked the beginning of a joking relationship between their two ethnic groups, which has survived to date. This could be a very classic example of how a difficult problem situation was used to put in place a mechanism for conflict resolution, an example that can serve us in the twenty-first century. Andaan' Siʋili also hears that Kumpati had advanced from Daboya in Gonjaland and occupied Lingbuŋ, but held his peace.

Zanjina sends Talɔli lan' Bukali [30], Tampiuŋ lana Birichim [32], Naantɔn' naa Suhu Biɛribo [33], ʒaŋ Mbanaa Laʋ' chee [34], Lingbuŋ lana Dasana [35], Tolin' naa Nadima [36], Savilugu naa Puu Samli [38], and Zangbalin' naa Yaʋiri yua [39], who all try in vain to convince Andaan' Siʋili to come to the King's aid. In the meanwhile, Kumpati was at Lingbuŋ, drinking and continually taunting the Dagombas to the effect that he was peerless in the whole of the Dagomba Kingdom: "What Dagomba woman can ever get the vagina to give birth to a man like he, Kumpati?"

Diyali lana Tisua [40] eventually succeeds in forcing Siʋili out of his self-imposed exile by invoking the spirits of the latter's parents in his presence before he could find words to vent his anger on the former, as was done to the previous emissaries. Andani's modus operandi was that he always swore by his deceased parents that he would not go to Zanjina's aid in the war against Kumpati before any of the emissaries could even announce their mission. Breaking an oath one has sworn that centered on the ancestors is a serious taboo, and so Andani's oaths had the effect of taking the wind out of the sails of the emissaries. That was why Tisua had to beat him by first invoking the spirits of the dead.

When Siʋili and his party arrive at Yani Zanjina reminds the former of the Nayiri's exhortation that he should forget the past and recognize Zanjina as King. Siʋili is entreated to support Zanjina, so that the latter's death he, Andani, would become King. Zanjina tells the assembly his death is imminent, and asks if they would let the son of a Gonja annex their fatherland. Andaan Siʋili hereafter tells Zanjina he, a commoner, could not lead titled persons to battle. In answer to this Zanjina confers the title, Siŋ' lana (chief of Siŋa), which had been the title of Siʋili's deceased brother, Siŋ lana Baakari, on him.

From here, Zaʋili's son, Andaan' Siʋili decides the might of his force would be too stong for Goliŋgoliŋ Kumpati alone. He needs to start from a distance and work towards Kumpati. He thus started his fighting from Konkombaland, through Mantili, Boguligu, Waambuŋ, Nasamba, and Tampiuŋ Waʋiri, killing all the earth priests who ruled over those areas. This was a rehearsal for the main task ahead. At the same time, his main foe had advanced deeper and deeper, till he got to Saŋ, near Yendi, the capital of Dagbaŋ. Here, legend has it that Andani used magical powers to keep Kumpati encamped at the Saŋ valley.

It was at this time Naa Zanjina died. Andaan' Siʋili sends messengers to Agbandi to see to the burial of the King and continues on his journey to meet the Gonja warrior.

Andaan Siʋili moves from Tampiuŋ Wuʋuri to Sakpɛʋu, where he engages in discourse with the Sakpɛʋu tindana, who informs Siʋili that it was the local market day, and they were celebrating. When asked the name of the market the tindana says it is called, *tarim baʋi zoo zuʋu* 'the common man perches on the hillside'. Siʋili takes offense, and gives the earth priest a poisonous concoction to drink, and he dies. He says from then onward, the name of the market would be *m ma niŋ mo'ʒee tabi luʋuli zuʋu* "my mother is the colored plant on the side", so that prominent as the colored plant is no one can miss seeing her, and that tolls from the market would be used for his mother's upkeep.

At the river Kulikpuni, he plants seven seeds, and tells his people that these are strange trees, and that it was he Siʋili planting them, and that the day anyone could tell what tree they were, that would be the day Dagbon would collapse. The legend is that those trees grew within a day, and three centuries on they still stand there. It is taboo for any Dagomba warriors to set eyes on them so they do well to avoid getting anywhere near there. Andani sends messengers to Kumpati to give him feed (sorghum) for his horse named *yɛla be biɛʋu* 'tomorrow shall be an eventful day'. Kumpati returns the messengers with insults, and tells him that he has barns full of grain, but he would not give him any. He would feed them to his own horse named, *m bi zaʋisi zuɲɔ* 'I don't mind them taking place today'. He also tells them his praise names are,

> i. Laringa yi kuli tam pia zuʋu, jaambona awei ni siʋisi o na
> Squirrel if just perch on platform clubs nine will bring-down it hither.
> If a squirrel rests on a high platform, nine clubs will bring it down
> ii. Tandɔʋu lɔŋ kum boli saa, saa mi ni bu o
> Ditch frog cry call rain, rain too will beat him
> The frog has called the rain; rain shall thrash it.

This mutual taunting game is akin to throwing down the gauntlet, a run down to the epic battle between the two giants. Andani issued the challenge and Kumpati accepted it. Kumpati also says he is the "nine clubs", and "the rain", that will put Andani "the frog" in his rightful place. These names are taunts that are meant to pour scorn on the Dagomba royal.

On different occasions Gonja and Dagomba women clash at the river side. Young men clash in the bush when they go to get hay for their horses. The Dagombas are victorious on all occasions. It was here *kun' yiʋisirili* "the drummer's call to the king to wake up" occurs. Namonaa Wɔb'laa Nyɔʋu Kun Dari had to be alert, to wake Siʋili up on the day of battle. This has been instituted in Dagbon, and drummers go to the palace at dawn on Mondays and Fridays to rouse the king, to get up to perform his stately duties. He alerts the King, who is symbolized by the Lion, that, *kunduŋ puʋisiri gbuʋinli bia napɔnkpaa ni o gbaai* 'the hyena is (on the heel of the lion), stalking the lion'. This tune has since then been the drum signal used to wake the Dagomba king up at dawn on Mondays and Fridays. The hyena is the prowling day with its challenges that try to sneak up on the King. Being the lion he is, he should beat the schemer and get his plans through. The clash of the giants takes place in the Saŋ Chirizaŋ valley, where Andani slays Kumpati.

To go back to Andaan' Siʋili's beginnings, Sonaa Wɔrigu gave birth to his mother Ziŋ naa, who is bethrothed to naa Zaʋili, and given the royal-wife-title Napaʋ Gɔrigu lana. She gives birth to Andani when all the other royal wives are away in the fields planting the early sorghum (*Siʋili ka' birili*), hence the name Siʋili "Lean Season". Gɔrigulana had given birth to a strong boy, a *tin' maana* (a nation builder) as well a *tin'saʋinda* (a nation wrecker), who already had teeth in his mouth at birth. A rational man is considered the one who works hard to build a nation, but has the capacity to destroy in his moments of 'madness'. At the naming ceremony the father says the child's name is *Man' daŋ biɛm (n tiligi saa mibu)* (I have overcome malice), *ka'bira bela zaŋ gu maŋa sivili* 'the little leftover grain is reserved for the lean season.' These become part of the young Andaan' Sivili's appellations.

After the epic clash Sivili decides to make Kumpati's daughter Puumaaya his wife. She declines, and is told that the spear that slays the old can also slay the young. She is taken into the royal house, under the title Gbanzaliŋ, and eventually gives birth to Andaan' Sivili's first son, Yamusah.

Lessons to Be Derived from the Poem

The story is a lesson in cultural education, it shows the importance of the spoken word, pride is scorned, the use to which wit/guile can be put, history and genesis of many cultural practices. Other lessons include instruction in etiquette and the importance of respect for elders, the consequences of disunity/ sibling rivalry versus one of unity between siblings, wit is rewarded, over-reaching oneself can lead to disaster (Zanjina had slighted all the senior princes, and they wouldn't help fight for the kingdom against Kumpati), and the introduction of Islam into Dagbaŋ. It is incredible the number of praise names I collected from this single epic story. These proverbial names encode many cultural elements, beliefs, and the general worldview of the people. Firstly, we get some insight into the workings of the Dagomba royal house. A King's wives must be of a kingly status too, so they must give them royal tiltles, as happened in the case of Zanjina's mother, Adisa Nanga, who becomes Napaɣ Taayili. If a man grows in stature so must his wife.

Metaphors in Performance

The metaphors at the core of the mythic processes serve to capture the emotions of the audience, both primary and secondary, moving them between the past and the present. This entrapment ties paradoxes and their unraveling within the performance, so that the audience waits to see how the riddles will be solved. How does the Mamprugu King resolve the impasse between the feuding Dagomba royals? This is a development each member of the audience is interested in. Plus, what do the proverbial names stand for? How related are 'the broad chest' and 'Zanjina' on the one hand; 'Dagbon and Mamprugu' and 'adornments' on the other, in the riddle/proverb "the broad chest shall take the adornments"; which is the praise name Zanjina chooses that gives him the coveted prize (see 16 under Table 6.1). The analogy reveals a description that paints the picture of a broad chested, strong Zanjina capable of using his strong personality to unite the two ethnic groups in the same way the chest brings robes together.

His boldness and courage fits the paradigm Maslow (1968) talks of, as traits that lead a person to realize his or her full potential. This tendency toward self-actualization has motivational force that is promoted by a supportive, evaluation-free environment."[11]

The royals are motivated by their desire to rise up to the high office, which each sees as the ultimate in life. Riches or educational attainment are not as valued as the *nam* 'royal title'. This goal is the stimulus that calls forth their reactions, and it is these pictures they present that become the story the griots will sing. The pictures, physical or mental, intrinsic or extrinsic, evoke opportunities for action that define self identity and various sources of value that motivate, and lead to a certain change in behavior.

The epic session as we see from these analyses is a composite of song, praise and communication. Because it lasts the whole night the artist is able to sing the praises of thousands of people, living and dead, bridging the present and the past, and also renewing bonds between the rulers and their subjects.

---

[11] See Steinberg and Ben-Zeev 2001: 285.

Chapter 7

CONCLUSIONS

> Music is a system of communication, and "… as a kind of language
> [it] is culturally rooted and socially enacted, [and its] purpose is to
> convey meanings"[1]

When humans communicate they give as well as gather information. The communication of the proverbial praise names we have come into contact with in this book leads us to a conclusion that the choosers of these names are driven by some goals when they make their choice. Each choice seeks to attract some affection, control others, or achieve simple pleasure in being able to make him- or herself heard by others. Hewes and Planalp (1982: 107) assert that interpersonal communication is guided by curiosity and the need for efficacy. The curiosity to explore into the realm of poetry and choose words as will effectively present one as an orator is of paramount importance to the *salima* genre. This is what has preserved the praise singing of Dagbon for so many centuries. We have also observed that the performance of praise songs/ singing fulfils both functional and aesthetic roles. There are contexts or occasions within which certain forms of praises are sung, but whatever the case the practice is viewed as one that has been bequeathed to the people by their ancestors. This legacy is interpreted and re-interpreted by each performer.

Salima, whether glossed as "folktales", "praises", or "accolades", are cherished in the lore of the Dagombas. Folktales are so important that there is sometimes a blurring of the boundaries between the two worlds, the fantastic animal world and the real world of humans. Language ascribed to animals in

---

[1] Reginald Byron (1995:1) on John Blacking.

the world of folktales gets animated in everyday speech, so that a cultivated orator is one who metaphorically sees things in terms of other things, that is, he speaks of humans and their interactions by employing animal imagery. More than half the praise names collected also exploit the animal metaphor to delineate their human bearers. Praise singing is alive: a living practice, in the Arnold van Gennep sense, with names that classify people or explain issues; do and perform actions; or report and describe events.

When one says *luŋa ni salim ma* it sets off the meanings, "a drummer will eulogize me", "a drummer will sing for me", "a drummer will tell my story for me". This "story" is the story of my life; one that started with my forebears and becomes a never-ending story, because I will live it and pass the torch on to my progeny. The praise name thus has both diachronic and synchronic dimensions. These two dimensions are both important in this Dagomba cosmology where the folk believe in both reincarnation and the presence of munificent ancestral spirits that linger around to protect their progeny and descendants. Recurrent themes that transcend time get worked and reworked into praise names, songs, and epic narrations. Themes of the mighty versus the weak, virtue versus vice, witchcraft, beneficence, among others, feature prominently.

Dagomba praise poetry is so full of myths and legends which deal with the supernatural that the boundary between human forebears and gods get blurred. In the narrative poetry these venerable ancestors have transcendental wisdom, engage in mystical behavior, and perform awesome activities. These god-like characters and their activities form the backdrop of contemporary beliefs. The drummer's modus operandum then, is that he reclaims these ancient myths in the context of contemporary artistic recreations and imbues the lives of his patrons with ancestral sanction. This artistry enables the performer's audience to find an "us" in an "other", even if it is a known fact that the living cannot be the same as the dead.

In whatever way a praise singer goes about his duties he has a regard for the "praisee's" face concerns by reminding him of the good past which belongs to him/her now. In the same breath he reminds patrons that if they do not want to lose face then they must live above reproach. In this twenty-first century, with democratic secular governance in Ghana, one would not expect traditional, ethnic-based government to occupy a central position in the people's lives. This is not the case, as the folk are so passionate about things that unite and identify them in terms of their ethnic background, be they Dagombas, Gonja, Asante, Ewe, etc., first and Ghanaian second. Royals will go to any lengths, including a resort to sorcery to achieve the "highest title" they can aspire to reach; one's target being the last title their father rose to. In Dagbon, as has been observed, one chooses praises one finds attractive, and gets associated to those previously chosen by their forebears. The titles become extensions of their very beings much in the same way as their personal names belong to them, and could be means by which magical spells could be hurled at them. The fear of being affected by magical spells from rivals guides the choice of names. One is careful not to evoke the anger of others by exhibiting excessive pride (*Hubris* in ancient Greek) when they take praise names. It is feared that wicked folk will cast magical spells on them and blame the ill that will befall the victim on choosing a name too big for him/ her.

At the outset I asked the question why people take these praise names if they have the potential to estrange people. Are these practices beneficial? Without a doubt, epics reflect the people's historical traditions, and unite the living with their past relations. Time is bridged, and thus people see themselves communing with generations gone by, and generations yet unborn.

The praises and histories define people and communities, and show the relations between geographic regions. The Dagombas trace ancestral relations with the Mossi of Burkina Faso, the Kussasi of North Eastern Ghana, and the Mamprusi and Nanumba of the Northern region of Ghana, through their common ancestor Gbewaa. This is corroborated by the oral traditions of the respective ethnic groups. Epics are thus invaluable in their role as a tool for the reconstruction of group history.

Another very important benefit is that, in their description of the lives of culture heroes drummers present a "heroic literature [that] conforms to set patterns of behavior reflective of the society's worldview", Johnson, 1992: 2. These are also found in the themes espoused by most praise names, positive or negative.

Also, they play an important role is the use in conflict resolution. For example, in the absence of central authority as in acephalous societies (e.g., among the Tiv of Northern Nigeria) blood lines recreated by folk epic narrators help to narrow people's differences. When disputants get aware of their family relationships they feel obliged to be at peace with each other. Griots are the folk who eventually reconcile conflicting accounts. At the Wuako Commission instituted in Ghana to investigate the murder of the Dagomba king the drummers were brought in to fulfill this role by reminding the disputing Abudu and Andani royal houses of their common history, and the decisions taken in past similar situations of succession disputes.

We have also seen how praise names and praise poetry has been used by the bards to initiate action. By praising or insulting a patron the praise singer can move them to act. Johnson (1992: 5) calls the griots the conscience of kings, saying that poets have followed warriors into battle singing to encourage them. Dagbon drummers have always reminded their patrons that those ancestors of theirs who fell in battle fell with their bards, so patrons owe them, the descendants of these tragic drummer-heroes, and cannot leave them uncared for. Another example of words moving kings to action is found in King Luro's wife's taunts about him being a cowardly nonentity lacking in willpower; who did not even know where his predecessor's (Dariʒiɛvu's) mortal remains were. This leads him to go to war with Dajia, the Gonja warrior, a battle that is still remembered as the one that pitched the two major ethnic groups of Northern Ghana against each other.

PRAISE NAMES AND DAGOMBA WORLD VIEW

Kant (1790) is credited as the one who first coined the term *Weltanschauung* that has now come to be the equivalent of the English word, *worldview*. This is a concept that emphasizes the power of the perception of the human mind. To Kant *Weltanschauung* roughly translates as, our intuition of the world that has been gained empirically. Both the German word and its English translation quickly evolved into significant terms in Europe and America. Orr (1844-1913) in 1891 defines worldview as "the widest view which the mind can take of things in the effort to grasp them together as a whole from the standpoint of some particular philosophy or theology." (See Naugle, 2004: 5).

Praise singing, like the folk narrative tradition of the Dagombas presents dramatis personae in a certain light, which mirrors the people's way of perceiving the world where the native's "...outlook on things, his *Weltanschauung*", that motivates him to study his environment (Malinowski (1922: 517). Praise names and the oral narratives in which they abound, no doubt provide an avenue for Dagombas to look out upon their universe. Synge (1992: xxxviii), Degh (1994), Glassie (1995: 34), El-Shamy (2005: 263) say that people's stories attempt to send us to the bottom of their tradition, a mark of their cultural continuity, and learning. In this scheme of things the stories told in Dagbon tie the self, others, and universe together in their telling. Their experiences merge, that is, there is a shared experience, which allows the human audience to identify with or conceptualize the events unfolding in the narratives. The Dagbon cosmos generally centers on geographic areas within the ethnic group's land borders. This is why personages have praise epithets of their villages/towns of origin being part of their appellations. Foster (1966) in Dundes 1972 equates worldview to cosmology, and this fades to values. This formulation thus perceives a worldview as one that expresses "the implicit conception of the natural and social universe which exists in a subconscious cognitive level . . ." (See Kearney 1975: 248).

Praise names like folk songs and tales are performances within particular cultural milieux that feed them. These help peoples present the world as they envisage it to be. This is the case with the praise poetry genre of Dagbon. Cultural practices are used as resources for naming, for example,

> Na' bin biɛɣu maani kuli, o ku zaŋ buɣuli.
> King mean performs funeral, he won't take shrine
> A greedy king inherits the property of the deceased, but not the responsibility that goes with it.

Here the practice of the family elder presiding over the funeral celebration of family members is the backdrop for this praise epithet which Naa Zanjina uses to lampoon the Mamprusi King who appropriates the property of Nakpanzong Tindana, who the latter pretends is his maternal uncle. He is supposed to be responsible for the family shrine but he fails to take on that responsibility.

Many praise epithets echo the complementarity of the two sexes, to drum home Dagombas' idea of sexuality. It takes a man and a woman to make a couple. See 2, 4, 11, 26, from Chapter 5

> i. Jɔɣu ni bini: Yo' zuɣu yi kuli mali viɛli waayo di yɛn kpela pani ni.
> Groin in thing: penis head if just clean beautiful how it will enter vagina in.
> A thing of the groin: no matter how cleansed the prepuce is, it is meant for the vagina.

> ii. Ziŋguya ku kpiɛli taba
> Clitorises won't wedge each other
> It takes a man a woman to make love

> iii. Pani Maliɛɣu ku firigi nuu, naɣila yɔli.
> Vulva mushroom NOT unstuck hand except penis
> The mushroom in the vagina is not uprooted with a hand, but a penis

iv. Dakɔli yoli ku luɣusi vɔli ni.
Bachelor penis won't scoop out hole in.
A bachelor shall also find love.

This is a society in which there is a division of labor according to gender. Each sex has a specific role assigned to it, and society will frown on it if this specification is not adhered to. Two persons of the same gender are barred from any sexual relationship. It is a man, for example, who initiates a relationship, and he makes love to a woman. In the act of love-making old-fashioned Dagombas perceive the woman as being made love to, and not being an equal partner in the enterprise.

In the esthetics and concept of what constitutes the beauty of a woman, we find the following represented in the names collected:

1. Gbalipina sɔŋ gbina, ka gbina niŋ pɔrilo.
Thighs help buttocks and buttocks do curvy.
Heavy thighs make the posterior curvier.

2. Paɣasaribihi wuhirila gbuna, ka nachimba be kambon waa ni.
Ladies show-off buttocks and young men be-in war dance.
While the young ladies are exhibiting beauty the brave men are ready for battle.

3. Gbin'chu'yalim ku gari bia.
Buttock-gourd-width won't surpass child.
The big posterior cannot be more important than a baby. (Beauty is meaningless without progeny).

A big posterior is considered one of the qualities of a beautiful woman, hence its choice as a referent in these proverbial names. Every man desires a curvy derier in a woman, but this should not be at the expense of the primary procreative function. When people marry their ultimate goal is to procreate, so that a beauty with no birth is non-desirous. We are advised to be duty conscious through this sexual imagery.

The praise epithets we have met in this work introduce us to many Dagomba folk ways and beliefs such as concept of family, witchcraft, and polygamy, and also, the acquisition of power through fair or foul means. The Dagomba concept of "family" is well demonstrated by the drummers when they sing the genealogies of their patrons. One person is said to have several fathers and mothers. All siblings of one's father are enumerated as one's father; and the same holds true for the mother's siblings as mother. In this world one never lacks for a parent, for if the biological parent passes away there are others to fill the void. The praise names of the fathers and mothers are heaped on the children at praise singing sessions. Also, when a new chief ascends to the throne he is described as the inheritor of the past rulers, their *dabuɣlana*. If a drummer addresses the current Kumbuŋ chief as *ŋun tumdi ka di viɛla dabuɣ lana*, "the one who has inherited if-you-do-good's home", for instance, he is alluding to a past Kumbuŋ chief, Simaayila. The current occupier need not be direct blood relations with the older chief, but the fact that they both occupied the throne brings them under the umbrella of one family.

The formula for praises that are of the nature, *B laɣim kɔbiga/ tuhili, X n gari* "X reigns supreme among a multitude of B", is There are X, Y . . . Z members of the set of {B = animals/ objects}. I am X; and I am the best among the lot. B = {X, Y. . . Z}: X^0, where X^0 means X is primus inter pares. This is the equation choosers of these names that espouse the hegemonic concept of being better than others have in mind when they come out with this category of names.

Including a living chief in an assembly of eminent ancestors is good incentive for him/her to strive hard to achieve higher laurels, or to live up to the accolades that have been used to address them. These are the positive-pricking names whose aim is to motivate. They emphasize the "us-ness" rather than a "me" and "them".

Some of the proverbial names we have examined seek to commodify otherness (see Hooks 2001: 424) for they espouse a hegemonic principle of the bearers, their family, or ethnic group being superior. *Kunduŋ kuri kpani ni o ŋme gbuɣima*, "A hyena has fashioned a spear to strike a lion", *puu suɣuli din ŋmɛlim ku paai naa Gbewaa bia zɔŋ* "No farm hut can ever be as big as the royal palace entrance hall", etc. These category emphasize the ultimate superiority of the animal/item that symbolize the king.

Drummers as we have seen use their praise sessions to offer advice and give direction to their patrons, but their lore can also sow seeds of discord, especially where their advice infringes others' interests. In his exortation, as found in the Naya Samban Luŋa (Appendix 5), Issah Zɔhi asks his patron to emulate Naɣ'biɛɣu and progress to be King. He reminds him that,

Nav'biɛʏu daa ʒini o ba gbaŋ kpalim nam ni,

Ka m bɔri ni a tɔʏisi o ʒini gbaŋ kpalim nam ni, Zɔya pakpaŋ bia Aburu bla,

O bayili mali yaa, o mayili di mali yaa, Nyankpani pakpaŋ bia Aburu bla.

Nav'biɛʏu progressed straight from being regent to king,

And I want you to move straight from regency to kingdom, Son of the princess from the Highlands,

His father's house is powerful, his mother's house is powerful, Son of the Nyankpani Princess, Aburu.

This type of entreaty has led to royals trying to annex thrones instead of waiting for their turns.

Closely related to this is Naa Abdulai Ɖmarigɔŋ's epithet,

Bia bi gbamdi ka chana.

Child does-not crawl but walk.

A child that walks without crawling.

which he chooses to poke fun at his competitors. He rose to become king in spite of the kingmaker's claim that he was not fit to be king, because it was alleged he had deformities, which thus disqualified him from occupying the Gbewaa throne. His cousin Kpatiŋ lana Ziblim was made regent, when Naa Mahamadu Bla died, in his place. The political authorities of the day influenced Abdulai Ɖmarigɔŋ's choice. He chooses the name therefore to pass on the message that like a child that did not crawl before walking, he rose to be king without first crawling through a lesser chieftaincy title. He is also the,

Saŋmari gɔŋ ku ʒini tiŋa.

Star curved won't sit ground.

The crescent that won't rest on earth, but is high up in the sky.

This crescent is one that will rise to the highest regions, places no one ever dreamt he would get to. There is a good dimension to these names though, that is, if one has a good game plan, one can always rise to the occasion, or even above everyone's expectations.

Virtuosity of storyteller resides in how sensitive they are to the images that effectively summon the feelings essential to the success of the performance, knowing how, and when to evoke, cluster, or scatter these images throughout the tale. An ongoing self-evaluation takes place in the performance. The drummer poet passes on a subtle threat to his patron's potential enemies that he not only has a strong paternal clan, but has an equally strong maternal clan when he comments that,

> O bayili mali yaa, o mayili di mali yaa, Nyankpani pakpaŋ bia Aburu bla.
> His father-house has power, his mother-house has power, Nyankpani female-regent son Aburu young.
> Young Aburu, son of the Nyankpani female regent has powerful paternal and maternal backgrounds.

The subtle message is that if the regent, whose mother is from the Kokomba ethnic group, is harmed by anyone his kin will seek revenge.

The salima genre has at its core a quest by its practitioners and target audiences to maintain a certain identity. When they take a praise name, Dagombas are primarily driven by their desire to maintain this link with deceased family members. Living members of the family take names so that they will be identified by those appellations, and then when they are dead they also become part of the family song which will be sung for their descendants.

The venerable leader is presented as a liberator and a unifying force. Also during epic decantation the bards use digressions to present commentaries and comparisons of living personalities to their forebears so that in the same breath they conjoin history and present day realities and cultural values.

As in many cultures the world over, African oral poets narrate royal genealogies with on-going commentary. In Africa poet-praise-singers use their elaborate drum sequences to organize the community's cultural history, so that through the songs,

> The history and legitimation of political power are expressed and cultural
> identity and values are affirmed.
> Belcher (1999: 187).

Luŋ Issah Zɔhi at Biɛɣu Naayo typifies this in his words (as in Appendix 1),

> We do not enumerate how a king courts women,
> We do not narrate how handsome a king is,
> But we narrate man's deeds

> You know, it is for the sake of those not present that
> drumming was instituted

It is how well bards are able to balance narrations and digressions that show their artistry. Also, as observed by Kofi Awoonor (see Kunene, M. et al 1976: 7) in a panel discussion on oral traditions, "Whatever new forces come into focus will be brought into the already existing format and used." So that that recent happenings are incorporated into older frames and recreated within ongoing traditions. This is an effort at creating a new awareness in the society. Recent narrations (in 2008) of exploits of Naa Yaakubu Andani (died in March 2002) by Luŋ Issah Zɔhi and Banvim Lunnaa Ibrahima, for instance, fit this latter category of new creations within old paradigms.

We cannot go back in history to undo the damage that old proverbial, abusive, and mocking names have done, but we can certainly discourage creating newer ones. Drummers are the chief architects of these potentially explosive praise epithets, and can nip them in the bud if conscientized about their unbefitting or conflict inviting potential.

Educational authorities should consider introducing the art into the school curriculum, so that pupils will get into the heart of the art, and their culture, and not look down upon the drummers' ways. The drummers will thus be seen in positive light, as tradition bearers, and not beggars or pestilent solicitors. Drum music is as entertaining as Sherif Ghale's, Bob Marley's or Michael Jackson's. We also need more academic inquiry into the practice in order to help popularize the art.

Putting festivals on the national calendar of important occasions, will give them a national character rather than just an anonymous 'tribal' celebration. The scattered regional festivals and performances that are found in them collectively make up a national monument, with the drummers and their craft serving to increase and diffuse knowledge, just as the Smithsonian does. This has the potential to attract both tourists and curious academic inquirers to the land.

Commenting on the place of contemporary Yoruba oral poets, Olatunji (1979: 193) says that they are now more independent economically, for power has slipped from chiefs to administrators and professionals, and virtuosic poets are well respected in the society and hardly perform unless invited. There are however many soloists who have not mastered the art and do not know enough, who chant to passersby for money. These are not as respected as the first group. Unlike his predecessor who usually chanted in praise of the chief and the establishment, the oral poet is now free to comment on the goings-on in the whole society. Seasoned poets like Luŋa Alhassan bemoan the practice of these artists who 'cheapen' themselves by playing for a pittance. He also decries the tendency of some performers singing songs that are profane, reveal ethnic secrets, or have the potential to incite violence. In this light, he asked me not to divulge the secret of some narrations. He also wouldn't sing at the court of any king who disrespects a drummer, irrespective of the economic attraction. These are issues critical to the way one can "objectively" present ethnographic investigations. How do I respect my informant's position without sacrificing ethnographic "truth"? He sees this as a real degeneration of the sacred art of their drummer ancestors. In this light, he asked me not to divulge the secret of some narrations.

LIMITATION

The book has largely been fed by an analysis of first hand data translated from the original Dagbani language. As with most translations, there is a major limitation because it is difficult to give a 'perfect' word for word translation for concepts and idioms from two different languages or cultures. The entextualized words can hardly carry the local idiom. This exercise, to me, is a starting point, and is open for further improvement, especially as proverbial language may be liable to several interpretations. Crapanzano (1986: 51) calls this problem of translation *Hermes' dilemma*, and like Hermes, I have tried to clarify something that is opaque. My interpretations are therefore provisional, and can be improved. Context, the circumstances or events that foreground or create the environment within which events exist or take place, is very crucial to fully understanding literature, especially performance situations. There are signs (especially audio and visual) that are used in the live performances, which could either not cannot be captured or were not understood. In recognizing the importance of the sign in communicating behavior, Volosinov (1973: 28) notes that "a sign is a particular material thing, but meaning is not a thing and cannot be isolated from the sign as if it were a piece of reality existing on its own apart from the sign". Praise-naming, like other human acts of communication, is a continuous chain of speech performances and not just monologic utterances that can be divorced from "verbal and actual contexts" and must always be analyzed in context. To make sense we needs must connect acts to other acts or embed them within others. What constitutes 'sense' is not a universal phenomenon; it is culturally determined. To interpret messages we need to have information about the specific 'context' and the key, in which particular acts are done (Duranti 1997: 227).

Stewart (1978: 85) argues that social discourses are framed dialogic situations that have audiences ready to exercise a certain degree of subjective realism. What the group of folk consider positive praise and love to hear might appear nonsensical or unpleasant to their rivals. Commonsense and nonsense are two socially determined notions that keep each other in check and help in situating whatever text we write or enact in its proper context. These ranges of interpretive procedures used in text construction are shaped by participants' past experiences with other forms of textuality. Intertextuality thus comes with the application of experiences from our social life to the unraveling event or text. Social life is an emergent textual phenomenon that people frame/interpret for themselves. In Stewart's words,

> When we lift language out of context, we gravitate towards a failed event called 'nonsense'. Context does not stand guard around the text of the situation, ready to block any leaks in meaning. Rather, it is emergent in the ongoingness of the situation, the 'flow' of reality-generating conversation.

When the 'said' relates in a certain way with a vast amount of the 'unsaid', auditors need to lean back onto their shared values for clues to interpret the message, for the textuality of texts gravitates from realistic representations towards irony and metafictions.

The important lesson learnt from my analyses is that it is not easy to pass judgment as to whether a praise epithet carries a positive or a negative message. Such judgment is made from a certain personal angle, often based on selfish interest. Those who favor the chooser of the epithet look to its positive side, and see the name as one that boosts the patron's ego, often failing to see any negative themes, if the name slanders or taunts others. My primary informant's plea thus captures my main theses of balancing the act, and publicly presenting only those aspects as will praise, but not incite to violence. New praise epithets need to be taken by newly enskinned chiefs to water down the venom that some epithets their forebears took for themselves.

Outsiders who have long been attracted to the festivals of song, poetry and dance, but have in recent years stayed away for fear of being caught in the crossfires of feuding Dagomba royals will be willing to return to the festivals if there is no political tension.

During my research I observed the celebration of the major Dagomba festivals of Buɣum, Damba, and the Muslim Eids. Funeral and marriage ceremonies also featured prominently on my schedule of events. I took advantage of these ceremonies to observe some rare performances of these praise uttering moments. Documenting these praise epithets will serve the useful purpose of whipping up the awareness of a cross section of the society to the rich pool of verbal artistry in the possession of the oral artists, the drummers. These virtuosic performers are not a nuisance, who 'extort' money from, or 'beg' patrons when the former presses the latter with poetry. They are an asset we will always rely upon to provide the indigenous and cultural contexts, that is, the background information we will need in order to better appreciate their art; whether we view them as aesthetic works of art for our entertainment, or as historical material for our information and education. If we communicate the message to drummers and their patrons that there is the need to channel poetry to positive ends, we would all be the better for it, and nothing can achieve this better than documenting this tradition for all to see its beauty.

ACKNOWLEDGMENTS

I am grateful to colleagues in the USA who read the original manuscript and provided critical but constructive comments. Their comments have greatly impacted this book. In particular, I would like to express sincerest thanks to Professor John McDowell, Professor Samuel Obeng, Professor Hasan El-Shamy and Professor Henry Glassie. I'm also grateful to my sponsors, and more especially to my family (wife and children).

BIBLIOGRAPHY

Abrahams. R.D. (1968). "Introductory Remarks to a Rhetorical Theory of Folklore." *Journal of American folklore*, 81:143-148.

Abrahams, R.D. (2000). "Personal Power and Social Restraint." In Parèdes, A. and Richard Bauman (eds). *Toward New Perspectives in Folklore*, 20-39. Bloomington: Trickster Press.

Agovi, K.E. (1987). "The philosophy of communication in traditional Ghanaian society: The literary and dramatic evidence." *Research Review* No. 5 (2) 1989, 52- 59.

Agyekum, G. (2002). *Yendi Chieftaincy Trials of 1987: A Clash Between State and Traditional Norms. Conflict Resolution through Judicial Action. Judgements, Proceedings and Miscellaneous.* Cantonments, Accra: Justice Trust Publications.

Agyekum, K. (1996). "Akan verbal taboos in the context of ethnography of Communication". M.Phil. Thesis. Norway: University of Trondheim.

Akoma, Chiji. (2007). Folklore in New World Black Fiction: Writing and the Oral Traditional Aesthetics. Columbus: The Ohio State University Press.

Alver, B. (2005). "Folkloristics: The Science about Tradition and Society." In Alan Dundes (ed.) Critical Concepts in Literary and Cultural Studies, Vol. 1, 43-52. New York: Routledge, Taylor and Francis Group.

Ansu-Kyeremeh, K. (2000). "Communicating *Nominatum*: Some Social Aspects of Bono Personal Names". In *Research Review* New Series Vol. 16, No. 2. IAS, Legon, 19-33.

Arhin, K. (1986). "Asante Praise Poems: The Ideology of Patrimonialism." In eHRAF Collection of Ethnography, Doc. Number 34.

Bakhtin, M. M. (1986). *Speech Genres and Other Late Essays*. Trans. Vern W. McGee. Caryl Emerson and Michael Holquist (eds). Austin, Texas: University of Texas Press.

Barber, K. (1991). *I Could Speak Until Tomorrow: Oriki, Women, and the Past in a Yoruba Town*. Washington, D.C.: Smithsonian Institution Press.

Barber, K. (1999). "Obscuring the Exegesis in African Oral Praise Poetry." In Duncan Brown (ed.) *Oral Literature and Performance in Southern Africa*, 27-49. Athens: Ohio University Press.

Bascom, W. R. (1953). "Folklore and Anthropology." In *Journal of American Folklore* 66, 283-290.

Bauman, R. (1975). "Verbal Art as Performance." In *American Anthropologist*, New Series, Vol. 77, No. 2, 290-311.

Bauman, R. (1984). *Verbal Art As Performance*. Illinois: Waveland Press Inc.

Bauman, R. (2004). *A World of Others' Words: Cross-Cultural perspectives on Intertextuality*. Malden, MA: Blackwell Publishing.

Bauman, R. (2007). "The Emergent Quality of Performance." In Monaghan, L. and Goodman, J. E. (eds.) *A Cultural Approach to Interpersonal Communication: Essential Readings*, 35-37. MA: Blackwell Publishing.

Belcher, S. (1999). *Epic Traditions of Africa*. Bloomington: Indiana University Press.

Belcher, S. (2004). "Epics: Overview." In Peek, P. M. and Kwesi Yankah (eds.) *African Folklore: An Encyclopedia*, 113-114. New York: Routledge.

Ben-Amos, D. (2000). "Towards a Definition of Folklore in Context." In Parèdes, A. and Richard Bauman (eds). *Toward New Perspectivesin Folklore*, 3-19. Bloomington: Trickster Press.

Biebuyck, D. P. (1978). "The African Heroic epic." In Oinas, F. J. (ed.) *Heroic Epic andSaga: An Introduction to the World's Great Folk Epics*, 336-367. Bloomington: Indiana University Press.

Boas, F. (2004). *Anthropology and Modern Life*. New Brunswick, N.J. : Transaction Publishers.

Byron, R. (1995). "The Ethnomusicology of John Blacking." In Blacking, J. *Music, Culture, and Experience*, 1 - 30. Chicago: University of Chicago Press.

Charry, E. (2000). "The Jeliya" in Mande Music: Traditional and Modern Music of the Maninka and Mandinka of Western Africa, 90-192. Chicago: University of Chicago Press.

Chernoff, J.M. (1979) African rhythm and African sensibility: Aesthetics and Social Actions in African Musical Idioms. Chicago: The University of Chicago Press.

Chernoff, J. M. (1997). "Music and Historical Consciousness among the Dagbamba of Ghana." In Enchanting Powers: Music in the World's Religions. Lawrence E. Sullivan (Ed). Cambridge: Harvard University Center for the Study of Religion, 91–120.

Connerton, P. (2007). How Societies Remember. New York: Cambridge University Press.

Crane, J. and Angrosino, M. (1974). Field Projects in Anthropology:A Student Handbook. Scott Forresman.

Crapanzano, V. (1986). "Hermes' Dilemma: The Masking of Subversion in Ethnographic Description." In Clifford, J. and George E. Marcus (eds.) Writing Culture: The Poetics of Ethnography. Berkeley: University of California Press.

Degh, L. (1994). "The Approach to Worldview in Folk Narrative Study." Western Folklore 53, 243-52.

DjeDje, J. C. (2008). Fiddling in West Africa: Touching the Spirit in Fulbe, Hausa, and Dagbamba Cultures. Indianapolis: Indiana University Press.

Duncan-Johnstone, A. (1930). "Minutes of the Conference of Dagbamba (Dagomba) Chiefs Held at Yendi from the 21st to the 29th November, 1930, to enquire into and Record the Constitution of the State of Dagbon."

Dundes, A. (1999). International Folkloristics. Lanham, Maryland: Rowman and Littlefield Publishers, Inc.

Dundes, A. (2000). "Folk Ideas as Units of Worldview." In Parèdes, A. and Richard Bauman (eds). Toward New Perspectives in Folklore,120–134. Bloomington: Trickster Press.

Duranti, A. (1997). Linguistic Anthropology. Cambridge: Cambridge University Press.

Edwards, W.F. (1979). "Speech Acts in Guyana: Communicating Ritual and Personal Insults." In Journal of Black Studies, Vol. 10, No. 1., 20-39.

El-Shamy, H. M. (1967). "Folkloric Behavior: A Theory for the Study of the Dynamics of Traditional Culture." Doctoral Disssertation, Department of Folklore and Ethnomusicology, Indiana University.

El-Shamy, H. (2004). Types of the Folktale in the Arab World: A Demographically Oriented Tale-Type Index. Bloomington: Indiana University Press.

El-Shamy, H. (2005). "Individuation". In Jane Garry and Hasan El-Shamy (ed.) *Archetypes and Motifs in Folklore and Literature, a Handbook*, 263-270. New York: M. E. Sharpe.

Eliade, M. (1968). *Myth and Reality*. Trask, W. R. (Trans. 1963). Reprint, New York: Harper and Row.

Fage, J. D. (1978). *A History of Africa*. London: Hutchinson and Co. Ltd.

Finnegan, R. (1970). *Oral literature in Africa*. London: Oxford University Press. "Ghana (1964) Special Report 'E'. Tribes in Ghana."

Finnegan, R. (2007). *The Oral and Beyond: Doing Things with Words in Africa*. Chicago: The University of Chicago Press.

Firth, R. (1974). "Verbal and Bodily Rituals of Greeting and Parting." In J.S. La Fontaine (ed.) *The Interpretation of Ritual: Essays in Honour of A. I. Richards*, 1-38. London: Tavistock.

Foley, J. M. (1986). "Tradition and the Collective Talent: Oral Epic, Textual Meaning and Receptionalist Theory." In *Cultural Anthropology*, Vol. 1, no. 2, 203-222.

Geertz, C. (1973). *The Interpretation of Cultures*. New York: Basic Books.

Glassie, H. (1995). *Passing the Time in Ballymenone*: *Culture and History of an Ulster Community*. Bloomington : Indiana University Press.

Goffman, E. (1955). "On Face Work. An Analysis of Ritual Elements in Social Interaction." In *Psychiatry* 18, 213-231.

Goffman, E. (1956). "The Nature of Deference and Demeanor." In *American Anthropologist*, New Series, Vol. 58, No. 3, 473-502.

Goodenough, W.H. (1956). "Componential Analysis and the Study of Meaning." *Language* 32 (1), 195-216.

Goody, E. (1972, 1974). "'Greetings," "Begging," and the Presentation of Respect'. In J.S. La Fontaine (ed.) *The Interpretation of Ritual: Essays in Honour of A. I. Richards*, 39-71. London: Tavistock.

Gramsci, A. (1999). "Observations on Folklore." In AlanDundes (ed.) *International Folkloristics*, 131-136.

Gunner, L. (1999). "*Remaking the Warrior?* The Role of Orality in the Liberation Struggle and in Post- Apartheid South Africa." In Duncan Brown (ed.) *Oral Literature and Performance in Southern Africa*, 50-59. Athens: Ohio University Press.

Hainsworth, J. B. (1981). "Ancient Greek." In Haito, A.T. (ed.) *Traditions of Heroic and Epic Poetry*. Volume One, 20-47. London: The Modern Humanities research Association.

Hammersley, M. (1992). *What's Wrong with Ethnography?* London: Routeledge.

Haugen, E. (1957). "The Semantics of Icelandic Orientation". *Word* 13 (3), 447- 459.

Hewes, D. E. and Planalp, S. (1982). "There Is Nothing as Useful as a Good Theory: The Influence of Social Knowledge on Interpersonal Communication." In Roloff, M. E. and Charles R. Berger (eds.) *Social Cognition and Communication*, 107-150. Beverly Hills: Sage Publications.

Hooks, B. (2001). "Eating the Other: Desire and Resistance." In Durham, M.G. and Douglas M. Keller (Eds.) (2001). *Media and Cultural Studies*, 424- 438. Malden, MA: Blackwell Publishing.

Hymes, D. (1968). "The Ethnography of Speaking." In *Readings in the Sociology ofLanguage*. Joshua Fishman, ed. The Hague: Mouton.

Hymes, D. (1975). "Breakthrough into Performance." In Dan Ben-Amos and Kenneth Goldsmith (eds.) *Folklore: Performance and Communication*, 11-74.

Hymes, D. (2000). "The Contribution of Folklore to Sociolinguistic Research" In Paredes, A. and Richard Bauman (eds). *Toward New Perspectives in Folklore*, 120-134. Bloomington: Trickster Press.

http://www.ghanaweb.com/GhanaHomePage/NewsArchive/artikel.php?ID=15 0139.

Iddi, D. (1968). *Field Notes: The Yendi Project Report No. 12a. The Ya Na of the Dagombas*. Legon, Accra: Institute of African Studies.

Innes, G. (1976). *Kaabu and Fuladu: Historical Narratives of the Gambian Mandinka*. London: University of London School of Oriental and African Studies, Redwood Burn Ltd.

Irvine, J. T. (1989). "When Talk Isn't Cheap: Language and Political Economy." In *American Ethnologist*, Vol. 16, No. 2, 248-267.

Jakobson, R. (1960). "Linguistics and Poetics". In Sebeok, T. A. (ed). *Style in Language*. Cambridge, Massachusetts: MIT Press.

Johnson, J. W. (1992). *The Epic of Son-Jara: A West African Tradition*. Bloomington: Indiana University Press.

Johnson, J. W. (1999). "The Dichotomy of Power and Authority in Mande Society and in the Epic of *Sunjata*." In Austen, R. A. (ed.) *In Search of Sunjata: The Mande Epic as History, Literature and Performance*, 9-23. Bloomington: Indiana University Press.

Joyce, J. (2004). "Epics: West African Epics." In Peek, P. M. and Kwesi Yankah (eds.) *African Folklore: An Encyclopedia*, 115-118. New York: Routledge.

Keenan, E. (1991). "Norm Makers, Norm breakers: Uses of Speech by Men and Women in a Malagasy Community." In Bauman, R. And Sherzer, J. (Eds.). *Explorations in the Ethnography of Speaking*, 125-143. Cambridge: Cambridge University Press.

Kinney, S. (1970). "Drummers in Dagbon: the Role of the Drummer in the Dagomba Festival." In *Ethnomusicology* 14, No. 2, 258-265.

Kunene, M., Daniel Kunene, and Kofi Awoonor (1976). "Panel on South African Oral Traditions" *Issue: A Journal of Opinion*, Vol. 6, No. 1, Proceedings of the Symposium on Contemporary African Literature and First African Literature Association Conference, 5-13.

Labov, W. (1966). *The Social Stratification of English in New York City.* Washington: Center for Applied Linguistics.

Leach, E. R. (1968). "Ritual." In *International Encyclopedia of the Social Sciences* 13.

Lasswell, H. D. (1949). "The Structure and Function of Communication in Society." In W. Schramm (ed.) *Mass Communications*. Illinois: University of Illinois Press.

Lawuyi, O. B. (1990). "Is Tortoise a Trickster?" *African Languages and Culture,* Vol. 3, 71-86.

Locke, D. (1990). *Drum Damba: Talking Drum Lessons.* Crown Point, Indiana: White Cliffs Media Company.

Locke, D. (2005). "Africa: Ewe, Mande, Dagbamba, Shona, BaAka." In Jeff Todd Titon (ed.) *Worlds of Music: An Introduction to the Music of the World's Peoples*. Shorter Version, Second Edition, 73- 121. Belmont, CA: Schirmer Thomson Learning.

Lubeck, P. (1968). *The Yendi Project: Patterns of Assimilation of Hausa Families in Dagomba.* Legon, Accra: Institute of African Studies.

Lyons, J. (1977). *Semantics* I. New York: Cambridge University Press.

Mahama, I. (2004). *History and Traditions of Dagbon.* Tamale, Ghana: GILLBT Printing Press.

Malinowski, B. (1922). *Argonauts of the Western Pacific: An account of Native Enterprise and Adventure in the Archipelagoes of Melanesian New Guinea.* New York: E.P. Dutton and Co.

Malinowski, B. (1946[1923]). "The problem of Meaning in Primitive Languages." In *The Meaning of Meaning*. Ogden, C. A. and I. A. Richards (eds.), 296-336. New York: Harcourt, Brace and World.

McDowell, J. H. (1981). "Toward a Semiotics of Nicknaming the Kamsá Example." In *Journal of American Folklore*, Vol. 94. No. 371, 1-18.

McDowell, J. H. (2000). *Poetry and Violence: The Ballad Tradition of Mexico's Costa Chica.* Champaign: University of Illinois Press.

McPhee, N. (1978). *The Book of Insults, Ancient and Modern: An amiable History of Insult, Invective, Imprecation and Incivility (literary, Political and Historical) Hurled through the Ages and Compiled as a Public Service.* New York: St. Martin's Press.

Naugle, D. (September 17, 2004) "Worldview: History, Theology, Implications." A paper Presented at the After Worldview Conference, Cornerstone University, Grand Rapids, Michigan.

Neeley, P. and Seidu, A. (1995). 'Pressing patrons with proverbs: Talking drums at the Tamale markets.' In *Research Review Supplement* 9. GILLBT Academic Seminar Week: Proceedings of 1994 Seminar, Tamale.

Newcomb, T. (1953). "An Approach to the Study of Communication Acts." In *Psychological Review* 60, 33-40.

Obeng, S. G. (1993). "Speaking the Unspeakable in Akan Discourse: A Linguistic Study." In *Papers in Ghanaian linguistics No. 9.* Linguistics Association of Ghana, 22-36.

Ogden, C. K. and Richards, I. A. (1923). *The Meaning of Meaning.* London: Routledge and Kegan Paul.

Olrik, A. (1999). "Epic Laws of Folk Narrative." In Alan Dundes (1999). (ed). *International Folkloristics*, 83-98. New York: Rowman and Littlefield Publishers, Inc.

Okpewho, I. (1992).*African Oral Literature: Backgrounds, Character, and Community.* Bloomington: Indiana University Press.

Olatunji, O. O. (1979). "The Yoruba Oral Poet and His Society." In *Research in African Literatures*, Vol. 10, No. 2, Special Issue on African Song, 179-207.

Olivier, E. and Riviere, H. (2001). "Reflections on Musical Categorization." In *Ethnomusicology* Vol. 45, No. 3, 480-488.

Oppong, C. (1973). *Growing up in Dagbon.* Accra: Ghana Publiching Press.

Parèdes, A. (1994). *With His Pistol in His Hand.* Austin: University of Texas Press.

Peirce, C. S. (1940). *The Philosophy of Peirce: Selected Writings.* J. S. Buchler (ed). London: K. Paul, Trench, Trubner and Co. Ltd.

Prussin, L. (1969). *Architecture in Northern Ghana: A Study of Forms and Functions.* Berkeley: University of California Press.

Rattray, R. S. (1928). "Some Aspects of West African Folk-lore." *Journal of the African Society,* Vol. xxviii, No. cix, 1-11.

Redfield, R. (1955). *The Little Community: Viewpoints for the Study of a Human Whole.* Chicago: The University of Chicago Press.

Richards, A. I. (1956). *Chisungu: A Girl's Initiation Ceremony among the Bemba of Northern Rhodesia.* London: Faber and Faber.

Salifu, A. 2000. "Communicating with the Chief: Ethnography of Royal Discourse in Dagbon". An M.Phil Book, University of Ghana, Legon.

Salifu, A. (2007). "Discursive Strategies at the Palace of the Yaa Naa, a Northern Ghanaian King." In Obeng, S. G. and Beverly A. S. Hartford (Eds.) *Issues in Intercultural Communication*, Vol 1, No. 1, 79-97. New York: Nova Science Publishers.

Salifu, A. (2008). "Finnegan, R. (2007). *The Oral and Beyond: Doing Things with Words in Africa.* Chicago: The University of Chicago Press, A review." In McDowell, J, and William F. Hansen (eds.) *Journal of Folklore Research,* posted March 26, 2008. http://www.indiana.edu/~jofr/reviews.php? id=69.

Saussure, F. de. (1971 [1915]). *Cours de Linguistique Générale.* Paris: Payot.

Scheub, H. (2002). "Myth, Music, Metaphor." In *The Poem in the Story: Music, Poetry and Narrative*, 173-229. Madison: The University of Wisconsin Press.

Seitel, P. (1980). *See so that We may See: Performances and Interpretations of Traditional Tales from Tanzania.* Bloomington: Indiana University Press.

Shannon, C. and W. Weaver (1949). *The Mathematical Theory of Communication.* Illinois: University of Illinois Press.

Shiloah, A. (1995). *Music in the World of Islam: A Socio-cultural Study.* Detroit: Wayne State University Press.

Small, C. (1987). Music of the Common Tongue: Survival and Celebration in Afro-American Music. Ondon: John Calder.

Smith, M. G. (1957). "The Social Functions and Meaning of Hausa Praise-Singing." In Africa: Journal of the International African Institute, Vol. 27, No. 1, 26-45.

Staniland. M. (1975). The Lions of Dagbon: Political Change in Northern Ghana. Cambridge: Cambridge University Press.

Stewart, S. (1978). *Nonsense: Aspects of Intertextuality in Folklore and Literature.* Baltimore: The Johns Hopkins University Press.

Stone, R. (2000). (ed.) *The Garland Handbook of African Music.* New York: Garland.

Steinberg, R. J. and Ben-Zeev, T. (2001).*Complex Cognition*. New York: Oxford University Press.

Synge, J. M. (1992). *The Aran Islands*. New York: Penguin Books.

Tarkka, L. (1993). *Intertextuality, Rhetorics and the Interpretation of Oral Poetry: A Case of Archived Orality*. In Anttonen, P. J. and Reinmund Kvideland. (1993). (ed). *Nordic Frontiers: Recent Issues in the Study of Modern Traditional Culture in the Nordic Countries*, 165-193.Turku: Nordic Institute of Folklore.

Thoms, W. J. (1972). *Three Notelets on Shakespeare*. New York: Haskell House Publishers.

Titon, J. T. (1998). *Powerhouse for God: Speech, Chant, and Song in an Appalachian Baptist Church*. Austin, Texas: University of Texas Press.

Titon, J.T. (2005). "The Music-Culture as a World of Music." In Jeff T. Titon (ed.) *Worlds of Music: An Introduction to the Music of the World's People*, 1-33. Belmont, CA: Schirmer Thomson Learning.

Turino, T. (1999). "Signs Identity, and Experience: A peircian Semiotic Theory for Music." In *Ethnomusicology*, Vol. 43, No. 2, 221-255.

Vansina, W. R. (1954). "Four Functions of Folklore." In *Journal of American Folklore* 67, 333-349.

Volosinov, V.N. (1973). *Marxism and the Philosophy of Language*. Trans. Ladislav Matejka and I. R. Titunik. Cambridge, Mass.: Harvard University Press.

Wafula, R.M. 2004. "Oratory: Political Oratory and its Use of Traditional Verbal Art." In *African Folklore. An Encyclopedia*. Peek, P.M. and Yankah, K. eds. New York: Routledge, 322-324.

White, H. (1988). "The Rhetoric of Interpretation and the Interpretation of Rhetoric." In *Poetics Today*, Vol. 9, No. 2, 253-274.

Yakubu, A. (2005). *The Abudu-Andani Crisis of Dagbon: A Historical and Legal Perspective of the Yendi Skin Affairs*. Accra: MPC Ltd.

Yankah, K. (1989). *The Proverb in the Context of Akan Rhetoric*. A Theory of Proverb Praxis. New York: Peter Lang Publishing.

Yankah, K. (1995). Speaking for the Chief: ɔkyeame and the Politics of Akan Royal Oratory. Bloomington: Indiana University Press.

INDEX